SaaS Development: Build Cloud-Based Applications

Master the Techniques of Software as a Service Using Python and AWS

Greyson Chesterfield

COPYRIGHT

DISCLAIMER

The information provided in this book is for general informational purposes only. All content in this book reflects the author's views and is based on their research, knowledge, and experiences. The author and publisher make no representations or warranties of any kind concerning the completeness, accuracy, reliability, suitability, or availability of the information contained herein.

This book is not intended to be a substitute for professional advice, diagnosis, or treatment. Readers should seek professional advice for any specific concerns or conditions. The author and publisher disclaim any liability or responsibility for any direct, indirect, incidental, or consequential loss or damage arising from the use of the information contained in this book.

Contents

Introduction to SaaS

What is SaaS?

Software as a Service (SaaS) is a cloud computing model where software applications are delivered over the internet as a service. Unlike traditional software that is installed on individual computers or on-premise servers, SaaS is hosted in the cloud and accessed through a web browser.

In the past, if a company wanted to use a specific software, it would have to purchase licenses, install the software on its own servers or local machines, and manage everything from software updates to security patches. With SaaS, all of that is handled by the service provider. The user simply pays for the software on a subscription basis and accesses it online.

Think of it like renting a house instead of buying one: you don't have to worry about maintenance or infrastructure; you just use the space when you need it and pay for it on a regular basis. Similarly, with SaaS, users don't worry about hosting, updates, or hardware, they just use the software as needed.

Examples of SaaS: Some of the most commonly used SaaS applications include email services, cloud storage, customer relationship management (CRM) systems, and project management tools. Here are a few of the most popular examples:

1. **Google Workspace**: Formerly known as G Suite, Google Workspace includes a suite of cloud-based

productivity tools like Gmail, Google Docs, Google Sheets, Google Drive, and Google Meet. Users can access these tools from any device with an internet connection. Google takes care of all infrastructure, software updates, security, and backups.

2. **Dropbox**: Dropbox is a cloud storage service that allows users to store and share files online. The platform enables users to sync files across different devices, making it easy to access documents, photos, and videos from anywhere.

3. **Slack**: Slack is a communication platform designed for teams and organizations to facilitate real-time messaging, file sharing, and collaboration. It can integrate with a wide range of other tools and is used by teams worldwide to stay connected and organized.

How SaaS Differs from Traditional Software

The main distinction between SaaS and traditional software lies in how it is accessed, deployed, and maintained:

- **Installation and Hosting**: Traditional software requires installation on personal computers or on local servers. Users need to ensure that the hardware is compatible and that the software is installed correctly. With SaaS, the software is hosted in the cloud, and users access it via a web browser. There's no need for local installation or maintenance.

- **Updates and Maintenance**: In traditional software, updates and maintenance are typically the responsibility of the end user or organization. This can be costly and time-consuming. SaaS providers handle all software updates and maintenance. Users automatically get the latest version without any effort on their part.

- **Licensing and Cost**: Traditional software often involves a hefty upfront cost for purchasing licenses, which can be a barrier for small businesses or individual users. SaaS, on the other hand, generally operates on a subscription model, where users pay a recurring fee (monthly or annually). This makes it more affordable and easier to scale as needed.

- **Scalability and Flexibility**: Scaling traditional software typically involves purchasing additional licenses, upgrading hardware, or paying for more on-premise infrastructure. Scaling SaaS is much easier. Users can simply adjust their subscription based on their needs, whether that means adding more users, increasing storage capacity, or enabling additional features.

Benefits of SaaS

1. Cost-Efficiency

One of the primary benefits of SaaS is its cost-efficiency. Traditional software often requires large upfront costs for purchasing licenses, paying for IT infrastructure, and maintaining the software. In contrast, SaaS operates on a subscription-based model, where users only pay for what they use. This makes it more accessible for small businesses and startups with limited budgets. Moreover, because the SaaS provider handles maintenance, security, and updates, users save money on IT staff and resources.

For example, a company using a SaaS CRM platform like Salesforce doesn't have to worry about hardware maintenance or server costs. The SaaS provider handles all that, leaving the company to focus on its core business.

Real-world Example: **Netflix**, originally a DVD rental service, switched to a SaaS-like model when it moved to streaming. By utilizing cloud computing, Netflix was able to reduce infrastructure costs and scale quickly as demand for content increased. This helped Netflix grow its user base rapidly, without the need for heavy capital investment in servers and data centers.

2. Scalability

Scalability is another key benefit of SaaS. Because the software is hosted in the cloud, it can easily scale to accommodate growing user bases, increased storage needs, or the addition of new features. Traditional software might require the purchase of additional hardware, new licenses, or significant updates to infrastructure as usage grows.

With SaaS, however, businesses can typically scale their subscriptions to match their needs. Want to add 10 more users to your team? It's as easy as clicking a button. Need more storage? Just upgrade your plan. This flexibility allows companies to adapt quickly to changing needs without worrying about the backend infrastructure.

Real-world Example: **Zoom** is another SaaS company that has benefited from cloud scalability. During the COVID-19 pandemic, Zoom saw an explosion in usage, particularly among businesses that were transitioning to remote work. The company's infrastructure, hosted in the cloud, allowed it to scale effortlessly to accommodate millions of new users and meet growing demand without downtime or delays.

3. Flexibility and Accessibility

SaaS applications are typically accessible from any device with an internet connection, which provides unparalleled flexibility. Whether employees are working from the office, at home, or on the go, they can access the tools they need to collaborate, communicate, and get work done.

This also opens up new possibilities for remote work, a trend that has accelerated in recent years. As more companies embrace flexible work arrangements, having cloud-based tools that can be accessed from anywhere is crucial.

Real-world Example: **Trello**, a popular project management tool, is used by teams around the world to organize tasks and collaborate. Because Trello is hosted in the cloud, users can access their boards from any device— be it a laptop, tablet, or phone—whether they're in the office, working from home, or traveling.

4. Ease of Use

SaaS applications are typically designed with user-friendliness in mind, which makes them easy to set up and use. Traditional software often requires an extensive installation process, and can involve steep learning curves for new users. With SaaS, since everything is hosted in the cloud, users can get started quickly without worrying about

configuring software or managing complex IT
infrastructure.

Furthermore, many SaaS providers offer extensive
customer support, tutorials, and documentation, which can
significantly reduce the learning curve.

Challenges in SaaS Development

Despite its many advantages, building and maintaining a
SaaS application comes with its own set of challenges.
Let's explore a few of the key issues developers and
businesses face in SaaS development.

1. Multi-Tenancy

One of the most significant challenges in SaaS
development is building a multi-tenant architecture. Multi-
tenancy refers to the ability of a single instance of a
software application to serve multiple customers (or
tenants), where each tenant's data is kept separate and
secure.

While multi-tenancy helps reduce costs (by sharing the
same application instance for multiple users), it also
introduces complexities around data isolation, security, and
scalability. Developers need to ensure that one tenant's data
cannot be accessed by another, while also optimizing the
application to handle potentially large amounts of user data.

Real-world Example: **Salesforce** handles multi-tenancy
by using a shared database and app instance for all
customers. Salesforce ensures that each tenant's data is

separated and encrypted, while also providing them with customization options specific to their business needs. This helps scale the platform without requiring individual infrastructure for each client.

2. Security

Security is always a critical concern in SaaS development. Since data is stored and processed in the cloud, ensuring that it is safe from unauthorized access is paramount. SaaS providers must invest in robust security measures, such as encryption, authentication, and firewalls, to protect sensitive data.

Moreover, since multiple tenants share the same application instance, it's essential to ensure that one tenant's data cannot be accessed by another. This requires the development of strict access control mechanisms, multi-factor authentication, and regular security audits.

Real-world Example: **Dropbox** experienced a data breach in 2012 when user credentials from another service were used to access Dropbox accounts. The company responded by improving its security measures, including implementing two-factor authentication (2FA) and strengthening encryption protocols.

3. Uptime and Reliability

SaaS applications are often mission-critical for businesses, meaning any downtime or service interruption can have a significant impact. Ensuring that the application is available 24/7 requires robust infrastructure, redundancy, and failover mechanisms.

Providers must ensure that their cloud environments are highly available and capable of recovering from failures quickly. This means implementing strategies like load balancing, backup systems, and data replication to minimize downtime.

Real-world Example: **Amazon Web Services (AWS)** itself is a SaaS provider that has experienced major outages in the past, such as the infamous 2017 outage that affected services like Netflix, Airbnb, and Slack. AWS learned from these incidents by further enhancing their systems for failover and redundancy.

4. Billing and Complexity

Managing subscription-based billing for a SaaS platform can become complex, especially as the customer base grows. Pricing models can vary widely—ranging from tiered pricing to usage-based pricing or freemium models—and each model comes with its own set of challenges in terms of tracking usage and managing subscriptions.

Additionally, handling issues like refunds, cancellations, and upgrades can add another layer of complexity to billing.

Real-world Example: **Spotify**, a SaaS music streaming platform, uses a freemium model where users can choose between a free version (with ads) or a premium subscription (ad-free). Managing this balance between free and paid users, while also offering multiple pricing tiers, requires sophisticated billing and subscription management systems.

SaaS has become an essential model for businesses of all sizes, offering cost-effective, scalable, and flexible solutions that can be accessed from anywhere in the world. Whether it's for communication, storage, or project management, SaaS provides a variety of tools that help teams collaborate, increase productivity, and reduce IT overhead.

However, as with any technology, SaaS development comes with its own set of challenges. Ensuring data security, managing multi-tenancy, maintaining uptime, and handling complex billing systems are just a few of the hurdles that SaaS developers must navigate.

By understanding these core principles and real-world examples, companies can better leverage SaaS to achieve success while avoiding common pitfalls.

Chapter 1: Fundamentals of Cloud Computing

Cloud computing has revolutionized the way businesses operate, develop, and deliver software. At its core, cloud computing allows organizations to access computing resources such as storage, processing power, and databases over the internet, instead of relying on physical hardware. This chapter will explore the essential concepts and deployment models of cloud computing, laying the groundwork for understanding how SaaS (Software as a Service) applications are built and delivered using cloud platforms like Amazon Web Services (AWS).

What is Cloud Computing?

Cloud computing refers to the delivery of various computing services—including servers, storage, databases, networking, software, and analytics—over the internet (the cloud). Instead of owning and maintaining physical data centers and servers, users can rent computing resources from cloud providers like AWS, Microsoft Azure, and Google Cloud. Cloud computing allows businesses to scale their infrastructure dynamically, pay only for what they use, and avoid the high capital expenditures associated with traditional IT setups.

In simpler terms, cloud computing is like renting a house instead of buying one. You don't have to worry about the upkeep, repairs, or buying new furniture every time you need more space. Instead, you pay a monthly fee for access to the resources you need, and you can increase or decrease the size of your house as required.

Key Characteristics of Cloud Computing:

1. **On-Demand Self-Service**: Users can provision computing resources as needed, without requiring human intervention from the cloud service provider.

2. **Broad Network Access**: Cloud services are available over the internet, which allows access from any device, anywhere, at any time.

3. **Resource Pooling**: Cloud providers pool their computing resources to serve multiple customers, using techniques such as multi-tenancy and virtualization.

4. **Elasticity**: Cloud resources can be scaled up or down quickly to meet changing demands. This is one of the primary reasons why cloud computing is so cost-effective.

5. **Measured Service**: Cloud computing is often billed based on usage, similar to how utilities like water or electricity are charged. This is referred to as a pay-as-you-go model.

Cloud platforms like **AWS**, **Google Cloud**, and **Microsoft Azure** offer the infrastructure and tools needed for developers to build and deploy applications in the cloud. These platforms provide the underlying services for a variety of use cases, including Software as a Service

(SaaS), Platform as a Service (PaaS), and Infrastructure as a Service (IaaS).

Cloud Deployment Models

When it comes to cloud computing, deployment models describe how the cloud infrastructure is set up and managed. There are three primary deployment models: Public Cloud, Private Cloud, and Hybrid Cloud. Each model has its benefits and ideal use cases depending on an organization's needs, security requirements, and resources.

1. Public Cloud

The **public cloud** is a cloud infrastructure that is owned and operated by a third-party cloud provider and made available to the general public. The cloud provider owns and maintains all the hardware and software required to deliver services. Customers can access resources and services via the internet on a pay-per-use basis.

Benefits of the public cloud:

- **Cost-Effective**: Because the resources are shared among multiple users (tenants), costs are lower.

- **Scalability**: Public clouds offer massive scalability since they are backed by the provider's large infrastructure.

- **No Maintenance**: The provider is responsible for maintaining the infrastructure, updates, and security, so businesses don't need dedicated IT staff for upkeep.

Real-World Example: **AWS**'s public cloud offerings like **EC2 (Elastic Compute Cloud)** and **S3 (Simple Storage Service)** provide flexible computing power and storage solutions to businesses worldwide. Companies can rent virtual machines (VMs) or storage on a per-hour or per-month basis, depending on their needs.

---

2. Private Cloud

A **private cloud** is a cloud environment dedicated to a single organization. It can be hosted on-premises or by a third-party provider. In this model, the cloud infrastructure is not shared with other organizations, and the cloud is managed either by the organization itself or by a third-party provider.

Benefits of a private cloud:

- **Customization**: Organizations have full control over the hardware, software, and security settings of their private cloud.

- **Security**: Since the infrastructure is isolated from other users, private clouds offer enhanced security and privacy, which is particularly important for industries with strict regulatory requirements (e.g., healthcare or finance).

- **Compliance**: A private cloud allows businesses to comply with data sovereignty and industry-specific regulations by keeping sensitive data within specific geographic regions or networks.

Real-World Example: Companies like **Netflix** and **Facebook** have private clouds to handle their data processing and storage needs. Netflix uses a combination of its private cloud infrastructure and AWS services to ensure high availability and performance for its streaming platform.

---

3. Hybrid Cloud

A **hybrid cloud** is a combination of both public and private cloud environments, allowing data and applications to be shared between them. This model provides the flexibility of using the public cloud for less-sensitive operations, while maintaining the private cloud for more critical workloads.

Benefits of a hybrid cloud:

- **Flexibility**: Businesses can leverage the best of both worlds by using the public cloud for scalability and the private cloud for sensitive workloads.

- **Cost Efficiency**: Hybrid clouds allow companies to optimize their infrastructure by balancing workloads between the public and private clouds.

- **Disaster Recovery**: Hybrid clouds provide enhanced disaster recovery options by allowing businesses to replicate data in both environments.

Real-World Example: **General Electric (GE)** uses a hybrid cloud to store sensitive industrial data in a private cloud while utilizing the public cloud for less-critical workloads. This enables them to optimize performance and minimize costs while maintaining security and compliance.

Cloud Service Models

Cloud computing services are typically categorized into three primary service models: **Software as a Service (SaaS)**, **Platform as a Service (PaaS)**, and **Infrastructure as a Service (IaaS)**. These models represent different levels of abstraction and control for the user. Understanding the differences between them is key to choosing the right cloud solution for your business.

1. Software as a Service (SaaS)

SaaS refers to software applications that are delivered over the internet, where the cloud provider manages everything from infrastructure to application updates. Users access the application through a web browser and typically pay a subscription fee.

When to Use SaaS: SaaS is ideal for businesses that need ready-to-use applications, like email, collaboration tools, or CRM systems, without worrying about the underlying infrastructure or maintenance.

Real-World Examples:

- **Google Workspace**: Includes Gmail, Google Docs, Google Drive, and other collaboration tools.

- **Dropbox**: A cloud storage service that enables file synchronization and sharing.

- **Salesforce**: A CRM platform that helps organizations manage customer relationships and sales processes.

---

2. Platform as a Service (PaaS)

PaaS provides a cloud-based platform for developing, running, and managing applications without the complexity of building and maintaining the underlying infrastructure. PaaS solutions include a range of tools and services for developers, such as databases, development frameworks, and application hosting.

When to Use PaaS: PaaS is ideal for developers who need to focus on coding and deploying applications without worrying about infrastructure management, such as provisioning servers, networking, and storage.

Real-World Examples in AWS:

- **AWS Elastic Beanstalk**: A PaaS offering that allows developers to deploy and manage web applications in various programming languages without managing the underlying hardware.

- **AWS Lambda**: A serverless compute service that allows developers to run code in response to events without provisioning servers.

- **AWS RDS (Relational Database Service)**: A managed database service that supports multiple database engines and automates tasks like backups, patching, and scaling.

---

3. Infrastructure as a Service (IaaS)

IaaS is the most basic level of cloud service. It provides virtualized computing resources such as virtual machines (VMs), storage, and networking, over the internet. Users are responsible for managing the operating system, applications, and data, while the cloud provider handles the underlying infrastructure.

When to Use IaaS: IaaS is ideal for businesses that want flexibility and control over their computing resources. IaaS allows businesses to scale up or down based on demand, and users have more control over configurations and settings.

Real-World Examples in AWS:

- **Amazon EC2 (Elastic Compute Cloud)**: Provides scalable computing capacity in the cloud, allowing users to rent virtual servers (instances) based on their needs.

- **Amazon S3 (Simple Storage Service)**: A scalable storage service used to store and retrieve any amount of data at any time.

- **Amazon VPC (Virtual Private Cloud)**: Allows users to create isolated networks within AWS, providing greater control over security and networking configurations.

Cloud computing is a transformative technology that has reshaped how businesses manage and deploy software applications. Whether using the flexibility of the public cloud, the security of the private cloud, or a hybrid model that combines both, cloud computing provides the scalability, efficiency, and reliability needed to support modern businesses. Understanding the key concepts—public, private, and hybrid cloud deployment models, as well as the different service models (SaaS, PaaS, and IaaS)—is essential for selecting the right cloud infrastructure for your organization.

By leveraging the cloud, businesses can minimize upfront capital investment, scale resources on-demand, and focus on innovation, all while taking advantage of cost-effective, secure, and reliable services. The next chapter will delve deeper into how these cloud models and services relate specifically to SaaS development, illustrating how businesses build, deploy, and scale their cloud-based applications on platforms like AWS.

Chapter 2:
Introduction to AWS

Amazon Web Services (AWS) is one of the leading cloud computing platforms in the world. Since its inception in 2006, AWS has transformed how businesses approach technology infrastructure, providing a suite of services that can be used to build, deploy, and scale applications without the need for large, upfront capital investments. In this chapter, we will explore an overview of AWS and its key services that are particularly useful for SaaS (Software as a Service) development. We will also look at AWS pricing and provide a step-by-step guide for getting started with AWS.

Overview of AWS and its Components

AWS is a comprehensive and widely adopted cloud platform that offers a vast array of services and tools to help businesses build scalable, reliable, and secure applications. It operates data centers around the globe, giving users access to computing power, storage, and other resources that can be scaled up or down based on demand. These resources are available via a pay-as-you-go model, allowing businesses to avoid the upfront costs associated with maintaining physical infrastructure.

Key Components of AWS:

- **Compute**: Services that provide the processing power for running applications and workloads.

- **Storage**: Services that enable the storage of data, such as databases, file storage, and backup solutions.

- **Networking**: Services to connect and manage infrastructure in the cloud.

- **Databases**: Managed database services for structured and unstructured data.

- **Machine Learning and AI**: Tools and services for building AI models and integrating machine learning capabilities into applications.

- **Developer Tools**: A suite of tools for developers to manage the entire application lifecycle, from code development to deployment.

- **Security and Identity**: Services to secure access, data, and resources in the cloud.

In the context of **SaaS development**, several key AWS services provide the core infrastructure needed to build, deploy, and scale SaaS applications. Let's take a closer look at the most important ones for SaaS.

Key AWS Services Useful for SaaS Development

1. **Amazon EC2 (Elastic Compute Cloud)**

Amazon EC2 is a core service in AWS that provides scalable computing capacity in the cloud. It allows users to rent virtual machines (VMs) on-demand, which can be configured with different amounts of CPU, memory, and storage. These virtual machines are known as **instances**, and they can run a variety of operating systems, including Linux and Windows.

How EC2 is used in SaaS:

- **Scalability**: EC2 instances can be scaled vertically (by increasing the instance size) or horizontally (by adding more instances).

- **Cost-effective**: EC2 offers on-demand pricing, reserved pricing (for long-term usage), and spot pricing (for unused capacity at a discounted rate).

- **Customizability**: Developers can choose the instance type based on their application's specific needs, such as compute-heavy or memory-intensive workloads.

Real-World Example: A SaaS application like **Zoom** could use EC2 instances to host virtual meeting rooms, enabling users to join meetings with varying degrees of demand based on user activity.

2. **Amazon S3 (Simple Storage Service)**

Amazon S3 is a scalable object storage service that allows users to store and retrieve any amount of data. It is ideal for storing files, images, videos, backups, and more. S3 is a critical component of many SaaS applications because it offers durability, availability, and security features at a low cost.

How S3 is used in SaaS:

- **Data Storage**: SaaS platforms often need to store large amounts of user-generated content (e.g., documents, media files).

- **Durability and Availability**: S3 provides 99.999999999% durability and is designed for high availability, ensuring that stored data is safe and easily accessible.

- **Security**: AWS offers fine-grained access control through IAM (Identity and Access Management) policies and encryption at rest and in transit.

Real-World Example: A SaaS-based photo-sharing app might store user photos in Amazon S3 to ensure scalability and durability, while also using access control to manage user permissions.

3. **AWS Lambda**

AWS Lambda is a serverless compute service that allows you to run code in response to events, without provisioning or managing servers. With Lambda, you can upload your code and specify an event trigger, such as an HTTP request via API Gateway or a file being uploaded to S3, and Lambda will execute the code automatically.

How Lambda is used in SaaS:

- **Event-Driven Architecture**: Lambda is ideal for SaaS applications that require event-driven workflows, such as processing payments, sending notifications, or generating reports.

- **Cost-Effective**: With Lambda, you only pay for the compute time used by your function, making it a highly cost-effective solution for occasional or unpredictable workloads.

- **Scalability**: Lambda automatically scales based on the number of events, so you don't need to worry about managing capacity.

Real-World Example: A SaaS application that processes user-uploaded data (like CSV files) could trigger an AWS Lambda function to parse the file, validate the contents, and store the data in a database.

---

4. **Amazon RDS (Relational Database Service)**

Amazon RDS is a managed relational database service that supports popular database engines such as MySQL, PostgreSQL, MariaDB, Oracle, and SQL Server. RDS simplifies database management by automating tasks like backups, patching, and scaling.

How RDS is used in SaaS:

- **Managed Databases**: SaaS applications often require relational databases to store user data, transactional records, and application configurations. RDS handles database management tasks, so developers can focus on building features.

- **Scaling**: RDS allows for vertical scaling (increasing database instance size) and horizontal scaling (read replicas) to support growing applications.

- **Backup and Recovery**: RDS provides automated backups, point-in-time recovery, and multi-Region replication for high availability.

Real-World Example: A SaaS CRM platform may use Amazon RDS to store customer records, sales data, and interaction history, ensuring data is highly available and easily queried.

---

5. **Amazon API Gateway**

Amazon API Gateway is a fully managed service for creating, deploying, and managing secure APIs. It enables developers to create RESTful APIs for their applications, which can be used to interact with backend services, such as databases, Lambda functions, or EC2 instances.

How API Gateway is used in SaaS:

- **API Management**: SaaS applications typically expose APIs for third-party integrations, mobile apps, or web frontends. API Gateway simplifies the process of creating, deploying, and monitoring APIs.

- **Security**: API Gateway offers built-in support for authorization mechanisms such as AWS IAM, Lambda authorizers, and Amazon Cognito for user authentication.

- **Scalability**: API Gateway can handle thousands of requests per second, making it an ideal choice for SaaS applications with high traffic.

Real-World Example: A SaaS-based e-commerce platform could use API Gateway to expose APIs for product catalog management, payment processing, and order fulfillment.

---

6. **Amazon CloudFront**

Amazon CloudFront is a Content Delivery Network (CDN) that speeds up the delivery of your content by caching it at edge locations around the world. CloudFront helps reduce latency by serving content closer to users, improving the performance of web applications.

How CloudFront is used in SaaS:

- **Static and Dynamic Content Delivery**: SaaS applications often serve static assets like images, videos, and stylesheets, as well as dynamic content like API responses. CloudFront accelerates the delivery of both types of content.

- **Low Latency**: By caching content at edge locations, CloudFront improves load times for users, especially those located far from your origin server.

- **Security**: CloudFront integrates with AWS Shield for DDoS protection and AWS WAF (Web Application Firewall) to block malicious traffic.

Real-World Example: A video streaming SaaS could use CloudFront to deliver video content globally, reducing buffering times and improving user experience.

AWS Pricing

One of the key advantages of AWS is its **pay-as-you-go** pricing model, which means you only pay for the services and resources that you actually use. AWS pricing can be complex, with various pricing models for different services, but understanding the basics is essential for managing costs effectively.

Understanding AWS Pricing Models:

- **On-Demand Pricing**: Pay for compute or storage resources by the hour or second, depending on the service.

- **Reserved Pricing**: Commit to using specific resources (like EC2 instances) for a 1- or 3-year term in exchange for a discounted rate.

- **Spot Pricing**: Purchase unused capacity at a significantly lower price, with the trade-off that the instances can be terminated with little notice.

Real-World Example:

- **AWS EC2**: Running an EC2 instance with a t2.micro instance type in the **on-demand** pricing model might cost around $0.0116 per hour. Over a month (720 hours), that comes to about $8.35. In contrast, using a **reserved instance** could cost around $5.60 per month, saving more than 30%.

Cost Comparison with Traditional Hosting:

- **Traditional Hosting**: If you were to host your web app on traditional servers, you'd need to purchase physical servers, pay for data center space, and handle maintenance. This can cost thousands of dollars upfront, and scaling can be slow and expensive.

- **AWS**: With AWS, you can start with an EC2 instance for less than $10/month and scale as needed. For a small web app, this can result in much lower costs compared to traditional hosting.

Getting Started with AWS

Before you can use AWS services, you'll need to create an AWS account and configure your environment. Here's a basic step-by-step guide to getting started with AWS.

1. **Create an AWS Account**: Visit the AWS website and sign up for an account. You'll need to provide a payment method, but AWS offers a **Free Tier** for

new users to explore a range of services at no cost (within certain usage limits).

2. **Set Up IAM Roles**: AWS Identity and Access Management (IAM) allows you to manage user permissions. Create IAM roles to securely control access to your AWS resources.

3. **Launch an EC2 Instance**:

   o Log into the AWS Management Console.

   o Navigate to EC2 and click **Launch Instance**.

   o Choose an AMI (Amazon Machine Image), select the instance type, configure security groups, and launch the instance.

4. **Deploy a Basic App**:

   o Once your EC2 instance is running, you can connect to it using SSH (for Linux-based instances) or RDP (for Windows).

   o Install your desired software stack (e.g., Apache, MySQL, PHP for a LAMP stack) and upload your app files.

AWS is an incredibly powerful and flexible platform for SaaS development, offering a wide range of services that cater to various aspects of building, deploying, and scaling cloud-based applications. By leveraging AWS services like EC2, S3, Lambda, RDS, API Gateway, and CloudFront, you can create a scalable, reliable, and secure SaaS application. Understanding AWS pricing and how to get started with the platform is crucial for optimizing both development and operational costs.

Chapter 3:
Introduction to Python
for SaaS Development

Python has become one of the most popular programming languages for developing Software as a Service (SaaS) applications. With its readability, scalability, and vast ecosystem of libraries and frameworks, Python offers a powerful foundation for building and deploying cloud-based applications. In this chapter, we will explore why Python is a great choice for SaaS development, delve into some basic Python concepts, and introduce popular web development frameworks like Flask and Django. We will also see a practical example of how Python can be used to build a simple CRUD application using Flask.

Why Python for SaaS?

Python has gained immense popularity in the tech world for several reasons, especially in the context of building SaaS applications. Let's break down why Python is a preferred choice for many developers and businesses:

1. Simplicity and Readability

One of Python's core features is its clean and readable syntax. Python's syntax is designed to be intuitive, with a strong emphasis on simplicity and minimalism. Unlike other programming languages that can be verbose or complex, Python allows developers to write code that is easy to read, understand, and maintain. This is particularly important for SaaS applications, which often require collaboration across development teams and frequent updates to features.

- **Example**: Building a small web scraper in Python can be done in just a few lines of code. This simplicity makes Python an excellent choice for quick prototyping and iterative development, which are common in SaaS applications.

2. Scalability

Scalability is a key requirement for SaaS applications. Python can scale to handle both small-scale applications as well as larger enterprise solutions. With the help of cloud infrastructure (like AWS) and Python's ability to integrate seamlessly with databases, message queues, and other services, Python-based applications can grow easily to meet increasing demands.

- **Example**: A Python-based SaaS application can start small with a few users and scale to accommodate millions, using horizontal scaling with cloud infrastructure such as AWS EC2 instances, load balancers, and containers (Docker).

3. Rich Ecosystem of Libraries and Frameworks

Python has a vibrant ecosystem of libraries and frameworks that simplify the development of SaaS applications.

Whether it's handling database operations, managing user authentication, sending emails, or creating RESTful APIs, there is a Python package for almost every need.

- **Popular Libraries**:
    - **Requests**: For making HTTP requests.
    - **SQLAlchemy**: For database ORM (Object-Relational Mapping).
    - **Celery**: For asynchronous task queues.
    - **Flask** and **Django**: For building web applications.

For SaaS development, these libraries and frameworks accelerate development and allow developers to focus on the unique business logic of their application rather than building everything from scratch.

4. Community Support

The Python community is large, active, and supportive. For SaaS developers, this is a huge advantage as it means you can easily find tutorials, forums, documentation, and solutions to common issues. The availability of a rich set of third-party packages, combined with the constant evolution of the language, helps developers address both common and complex use cases.

Basic Python Concepts

Before diving deeper into using Python for SaaS development, let's first cover some basic Python concepts that are essential for understanding how to build applications. We will go over variables, data structures, control flow, and functions.

1. Variables

Variables in Python are used to store data values. Python does not require explicit data type declarations, as it is dynamically typed. This makes it easy to work with variables without needing to worry about their data types.

python

```python
# Example of variables in Python
name = "Alice"  # String variable
age = 30       # Integer variable
height = 5.7    # Float variable
is_active = True # Boolean variable
```

2. Data Structures

Python provides several built-in data structures that are commonly used in SaaS development. These include lists, dictionaries, tuples, and sets.

- **Lists**: Ordered, mutable collections of items.

python

```python
fruits = ["apple", "banana", "cherry"]
fruits.append("orange")  # Adding an item to the list
```

- **Dictionaries**: Unordered collections of key-value pairs.

python

```python
user = {"name": "Alice", "age": 30, "city": "New York"}
print(user["name"])  # Accessing dictionary values by key
```

- **Tuples**: Ordered, immutable collections of items.

python

```python
point = (3, 4)  # Tuple for representing a point in 2D space
```

- **Sets**: Unordered collections with no duplicate values.

python

```python
numbers = {1, 2, 3, 4}
numbers.add(5)  # Adding an item to the set
```

3. Control Flow

Control flow structures allow you to define the logic of your application based on conditions (if-else), loops (for, while), and function calls.

- **If-else**: Conditional statements that execute different code based on a condition.

python

```python
if age >= 18:
    print("Adult")
else:
    print("Minor")
```

- **For loop**: Iterate over a sequence (list, tuple, string, etc.).

python

```python
for fruit in fruits:
    print(fruit)
```

- **While loop**: Repeatedly execute a block of code as long as a condition is true.

python

```python
counter = 0
while counter < 5:
```

```
    print(counter)

    counter += 1
```

4. Functions

Functions are reusable blocks of code that perform specific tasks. In SaaS applications, functions are commonly used to handle repetitive tasks, such as user authentication, data validation, or sending notifications.

python

```python
def greet_user(name):
    return f"Hello, {name}!"


# Calling the function
print(greet_user("Alice"))
```

Web Development Frameworks in Python

When it comes to building web applications for SaaS, Python offers two primary frameworks: **Flask** and **Django**. Both are popular choices for building robust, scalable web applications, but they differ in complexity and flexibility.

1. Flask

Flask is a lightweight and flexible micro-framework that is often used for small-to-medium-sized web applications. Flask gives developers full control over how they structure their application, providing the core functionality to get a web app running, but leaving the rest up to the developer. Flask is ideal for applications that need flexibility or a small footprint.

Core Features of Flask:

- Minimalist, with no built-in database or form validation tools.

- Highly flexible, allowing you to choose your libraries and tools.

- Best for small applications or those that need fine-tuned control.

Real-World Example: Building a simple **CRUD (Create, Read, Update, Delete)** application with Flask.

Steps:

1. Install Flask:

bash

```
pip install Flask
```

2. Create a app.py file for the web app:

python

```
from flask import Flask, request, jsonify
```

```python
app = Flask(__name__)

users = []

@app.route("/users", methods=["POST"])
def create_user():
    user_data = request.get_json()
    users.append(user_data)
    return jsonify(user_data), 201

@app.route("/users", methods=["GET"])
def get_users():
    return jsonify(users), 200

@app.route("/users/<int:user_id>", methods=["GET"])
def get_user(user_id):
    user = users[user_id]
    return jsonify(user), 200

@app.route("/users/<int:user_id>", methods=["PUT"])
def update_user(user_id):
```

```python
    user_data = request.get_json()
    users[user_id] = user_data
    return jsonify(user_data), 200


@app.route("/users/<int:user_id>", methods=["DELETE"])
def delete_user(user_id):
    users.pop(user_id)
    return '', 204


if __name__ == "__main__":
    app.run(debug=True)
```

3. Run the application:

bash

```bash
python app.py
```

In this example, we create a simple API with endpoints for creating, reading, updating, and deleting user information. This can be easily expanded and modified for real-world SaaS applications.

2. Django

Django is a full-fledged web framework that includes everything you need to build a web application, including an ORM (Object-Relational Mapping) system for databases, form validation, and built-in authentication.

Django is ideal for larger applications where you need a more opinionated, structured approach to development.

Core Features of Django:

- Includes built-in tools for authentication, database management, and user management.

- Strong community support and a large set of reusable components.

- Best for complex applications with multiple users, features, and components.

Real-World Example: Building a **User Authentication System** using Django.

Django's built-in tools allow developers to quickly set up user registration, login, and authentication with minimal code. This makes Django an excellent choice for SaaS applications that require robust user management features.

Python is a highly versatile and powerful language that is well-suited for SaaS development. Its simplicity, scalability, rich ecosystem of libraries, and strong community support make it an excellent choice for building cloud-based applications. Understanding the basics of Python, along with frameworks like Flask and Django, can empower developers to rapidly build, deploy, and scale SaaS applications. Whether you are developing a lightweight application using Flask or a more complex enterprise-grade solution with Django, Python provides the tools and flexibility to meet your needs.

Chapter 4: Designing a SaaS Application

Designing a Software as a Service (SaaS) application involves a series of steps, from structuring the architecture to choosing the right technology stack, designing the database schema, implementing security measures, and ensuring the app can scale with increasing users. This chapter will explore the key components that make up a typical SaaS application architecture, dive into database choices, explain how to build the backend using Python, and discuss the importance of security in SaaS development. Along the way, we will illustrate concepts using real-world examples, helping you design your own scalable and secure SaaS application.

Architecture of a SaaS Application

A SaaS application is typically designed to operate in a cloud environment, offering services to users on a subscription or pay-as-you-go basis. The architecture of a SaaS application can be broken down into several key components, which we will explore in detail below.

1. Key Components of SaaS Architecture

Frontend

The frontend of a SaaS application refers to the user-facing part of the application that interacts directly with the end users. It typically includes the web interface or mobile interface where users access the features and data of the application.

- **Technologies**: The frontend is usually built with HTML, CSS, and JavaScript. Frameworks like React, Angular, or Vue.js are often used to build interactive user interfaces.

- **Example**: In a SaaS application like Dropbox, the frontend includes the file upload, sharing, and organizational features, all of which are powered by JavaScript and communicate with the backend to retrieve and manipulate user data.

Backend

The backend handles the core business logic, data processing, and communication with databases or third-party services. It acts as the server-side of the application, serving requests from the frontend, performing calculations, and returning data.

- **Technologies**: The backend for SaaS applications can be built using several programming languages and frameworks. For example, Python (Flask or Django) is commonly used for building web servers and APIs that process requests and return data to the frontend.

- **Example**: In a SaaS application like Slack, the backend processes real-time messages, handles notifications, and stores user data such as messages and user preferences.

Database

The database is where all of the data, such as user information, files, preferences, and other application data, is stored. The database must be scalable, reliable, and capable of handling multiple tenants in a SaaS application.

- **Technologies**: SaaS applications commonly use relational databases (e.g., PostgreSQL, MySQL) or non-relational databases (e.g., MongoDB, DynamoDB) depending on the application's requirements.

- **Example**: In a SaaS application like Google Workspace, the database stores user profiles, documents, settings, and configurations.

Security

Security is a crucial component of any SaaS application, as sensitive user data must be protected from unauthorized access. Implementing the right security protocols is essential for maintaining user trust and compliance with regulations like GDPR and HIPAA.

- **Technologies**: Common security practices include encryption of data in transit and at rest, two-factor authentication, role-based access controls (RBAC), and secure authentication protocols (e.g., OAuth, JWT).

- **Example**: In a SaaS application like Stripe (a payment processing service), encryption and secure payment tokenization are used to protect sensitive credit card information.

2. Multi-Tenant Architecture

A multi-tenant architecture allows a single instance of an application to serve multiple customers, or tenants, while maintaining data isolation between them. This is a fundamental design choice for most SaaS applications because it enables efficient use of resources and reduces costs.

Key Features:

- **Single Application Instance**: A multi-tenant system runs one application for all users, rather than a separate instance for each tenant.

- **Data Isolation**: Although tenants share the same application resources, their data is kept isolated. This can be achieved through logical separation in the database.

Example:

- **Simplified Multi-Tenant Database Design**: Consider a SaaS application that allows businesses to manage employee records. In a multi-tenant architecture, each business (tenant) will have its own set of employee records. These can be stored in a single database with an additional tenant_id column that uniquely identifies which tenant each record belongs to.

sql

```sql
CREATE TABLE employees (
    employee_id INT PRIMARY KEY,
    tenant_id INT,
```

first_name VARCHAR(100),

last_name VARCHAR(100),

position VARCHAR(100),

FOREIGN KEY (tenant_id) REFERENCES tenants(tenant_id)

);

In this design, the tenant_id ensures that each tenant's data is logically separated, even though it's stored in the same table.

Database Choices for SaaS

When building a SaaS application, choosing the right type of database is crucial. The choice largely depends on the nature of the data, scalability needs, and the desired level of flexibility.

1. Relational Databases (SQL)

Relational databases, such as **PostgreSQL** and **MySQL**, are widely used in SaaS applications. They use structured query language (SQL) to manage and manipulate data. Relational databases are ideal for applications that require strong data integrity and complex queries.

Advantages:

- **ACID Compliance**: Ensures that all database transactions are processed reliably.

- **Structured Data**: Ideal for applications that require predefined schemas, such as user management or accounting systems.

- **Example**: A SaaS application like Salesforce uses a relational database to store customer records, sales data, and reports in a structured format.

When to Use Relational Databases:

- You need to handle complex queries with JOIN operations.

- Your data structure is well-defined and doesn't change often.

- You need strong consistency guarantees for transaction management.

2. Non-Relational Databases (NoSQL)

Non-relational databases, such as **MongoDB** and **DynamoDB**, offer flexibility in how data is stored. These databases don't require a predefined schema, making them a good choice for applications with unstructured or semi-structured data.

Advantages:

- **Scalability**: NoSQL databases are designed to scale horizontally, making them ideal for handling large volumes of data across multiple servers.

- **Flexibility**: Data can be stored in a variety of formats (e.g., JSON, BSON), which allows for more flexibility in handling different types of data.

- **Example**: A SaaS application like MongoDB Atlas uses MongoDB to store documents (e.g., JSON-like objects), making it flexible to store diverse datasets like user preferences or logs.

When to Use Non-Relational Databases:

- Your application needs to scale rapidly and handle large amounts of unstructured data.

- The structure of your data is likely to evolve over time.

- You need fast read and write performance with low latency.

3. Multi-Tenant Database Design

In a multi-tenant application, managing how tenants' data is stored in the database is crucial. One common approach is to use **shared databases with tenant isolation**, where the application stores all tenant data in a single database, but each tenant's data is logically isolated by using a tenant identifier (tenant_id).

Here's an example of how you can store user data in a multi-tenant environment:

- **Tenant-Specific Data**: Each user's data is stored in the same database, but each row has a tenant_id field to indicate which tenant the data belongs to.

- **Shared Schema vs. Separate Schema**: Some SaaS applications use a **shared schema** where all tenants' data lives in the same tables (as shown in the example earlier), while others opt for **separate schemas** for each tenant, providing stricter data isolation.

Building the Backend with Python

Now that we have a good understanding of SaaS architecture and database choices, let's dive into building the backend for a SaaS application using Python. In this section, we will explore how to build RESTful APIs with **Flask** or **Django** to handle the core functionality of your SaaS app.

1. Introduction to Building RESTful APIs with Flask or Django

A RESTful API allows the frontend of the SaaS application to communicate with the backend. REST (Representational State Transfer) is an architectural style that provides a simple way to interact with resources via standard HTTP methods (GET, POST, PUT, DELETE).

- **Flask**: Flask is a micro-framework for Python, perfect for small to medium applications. It is flexible, lightweight, and allows you to build APIs quickly.

- **Django**: Django is a full-fledged web framework that comes with built-in features like an ORM, authentication, and admin panels, making it better suited for larger applications.

2. Example: Building an API for User Authentication

In this section, we will walk through building a simple API for managing user authentication using **JWT (JSON Web Tokens)** for secure token-based authentication.

Flask Example for User Authentication:

1. Install required libraries:

```bash
pip install Flask Flask-JWT-Extended
```

2. Create a basic Flask app (app.py):

```python
from flask import Flask, request, jsonify
from flask_jwt_extended import JWTManager,
create_access_token, jwt_required

app = Flask(__name__)
app.config['JWT_SECRET_KEY'] = 'your_secret_key'
jwt = JWTManager(app)

users = {"user1": "password123"}

@app.route('/login', methods=['POST'])
def login():
    username = request.json.get('username')
    password = request.json.get('password')
    if username in users and users[username] == password:
        token = create_access_token(identity=username)
```

```python
    return jsonify(access_token=token)

    return jsonify({"msg": "Bad username or password"}),
401


@app.route('/protected', methods=['GET'])

@jwt_required()

def protected():

    return jsonify(message="This is a protected route")


if __name__ == '__main__':

    app.run(debug=True)
```

In this simple Flask application:

- The /login route allows users to authenticate using a username and password.

- If authentication is successful, an access token is generated and sent back to the user.

- The /protected route is a protected endpoint that requires the user to send a valid JWT token.

Security in SaaS

Security is one of the most important aspects of building any SaaS application. As a SaaS provider, you are responsible for protecting your users' data and ensuring the integrity and confidentiality of the information they entrust to you.

1. Authentication

OAuth and **JWT** are two widely used methods for handling authentication in modern web applications. OAuth is an authorization framework that allows third-party services to securely access user data, while JWT is a compact, URL-safe token format used to securely transmit information between the client and server.

- **JWT** allows you to securely transmit information using a compact, signed token.
- **OAuth** is used for secure delegation of access to resources.

Example:

- In a SaaS application like GitHub, OAuth is used to allow users to sign in using their Google or Facebook credentials.

2. Encryption

Encryption ensures that sensitive data is protected both in transit (over the network) and at rest (in the database). Common encryption protocols include **TLS (Transport Layer Security)** for data in transit and **AES (Advanced Encryption Standard)** for data at rest.

Example:

- In a payment SaaS like Stripe, all payment transactions are encrypted using SSL/TLS to ensure that card details are not exposed during transmission.

Designing a SaaS application requires careful planning, especially when it comes to architecture, database choices, and security. In this chapter, we explored the fundamental components of a SaaS app, such as frontend, backend, database design, and security. We also discussed how to build a backend using Python and implement authentication and encryption strategies to ensure the integrity and security of user data.

As you progress in your SaaS journey, remember that building scalable, secure, and high-performance applications requires not just technical expertise but also a deep understanding of your users' needs and how to meet those needs efficiently. Keep exploring, building, and iterating—this is how great SaaS applications are born.

Chapter 5: Deploying Your SaaS Application on AWS

Once you've designed and developed your SaaS application, the next crucial step is deployment. Deploying your application on the cloud brings with it a host of benefits such as scalability, cost efficiency, and availability. Amazon Web Services (AWS) offers a powerful set of tools and services that enable you to deploy, manage, and scale your SaaS application with ease.

In this chapter, we will walk through the steps required to deploy your SaaS application on AWS, covering how to set up AWS for deployment, manage your database with Amazon RDS, and scale and monitor your application using AWS services like Elastic Load Balancer (ELB) and CloudWatch.

Setting Up AWS for Deployment

AWS provides a wide range of services for deploying applications, and one of the most straightforward ways to deploy web applications is through **AWS Elastic Beanstalk**. Elastic Beanstalk is a Platform-as-a-Service (PaaS) solution that abstracts much of the complexity of deploying applications, letting you focus more on writing code rather than managing the underlying infrastructure.

Using Elastic Beanstalk for Python Applications

Elastic Beanstalk automatically handles the deployment, from provisioning EC2 instances and load balancers to managing application updates. It supports multiple programming languages, including Python, and integrates seamlessly with other AWS services like RDS, S3, and CloudWatch.

Step-by-Step Guide to Deploy a Flask App on Elastic Beanstalk

Let's walk through deploying a simple **Flask** web application on AWS Elastic Beanstalk.

1. **Prerequisites**:

   o   An active AWS account.

   o   AWS CLI installed and configured on your local machine.

   o   Elastic Beanstalk CLI (eb) installed.

   o   Python application ready for deployment (e.g., a simple Flask app).

2. **Prepare Your Application for Deployment**: First, make sure your Flask app has all the necessary files for deployment, such as a requirements.txt for dependencies and a Procfile to specify the application start command.

   o   Create a requirements.txt by running:

bash

pip freeze > requirements.txt

      o   Create a Procfile (no extension) with the
           following content:

makefile

web: gunicorn application:app

This tells Elastic Beanstalk to use Gunicorn (a production-ready WSGI server) to serve the Flask app.

3. **Initialize Elastic Beanstalk**: In your project
   directory, run the following command to initialize
   your Elastic Beanstalk environment:

bash

eb init -p python-3.x my-flask-app

This will configure your app for deployment and prompt you for your AWS region and other settings.

4. **Create and Deploy the Environment**: Run the
   following commands to create an environment and
   deploy the app to Elastic Beanstalk:

bash

eb create my-flask-app-env

eb deploy

Elastic Beanstalk will handle provisioning the necessary resources, such as EC2 instances and load balancers, and deploy your application automatically.

5. **Accessing Your Application**: After deployment is complete, Elastic Beanstalk will provide a URL to access your Flask app. You can open this URL in a browser to see your deployed app live.

AWS RDS for Database Management

In a SaaS application, the database is a central component. Amazon Relational Database Service (RDS) simplifies the setup, operation, and scaling of a relational database in the cloud. AWS RDS supports popular database engines like MySQL, PostgreSQL, SQL Server, MariaDB, and Oracle.

Setting Up AWS RDS for Your Application

In this section, we will focus on how to set up Amazon RDS with PostgreSQL and connect it to your Flask or Django app. PostgreSQL is a powerful open-source relational database that is highly suitable for SaaS applications due to its scalability, extensibility, and support for complex queries.

Step-by-Step Guide to Setting Up PostgreSQL with RDS

1. **Create an RDS Instance**:
   - Log in to the AWS Management Console and navigate to the **RDS** service.

- Click on **Create Database**, and choose **PostgreSQL** as the engine.

- Select **Standard Create** and configure the database instance with your desired settings (e.g., instance size, storage type, and security group).

- Set the **DB instance identifier**, **Master username**, and **Master password**.

2. **Configure Security Group**:

   - During setup, make sure the RDS instance's security group allows inbound connections from your application's IP address or security group.

   - You can modify the security group in the **VPC** section to open port 5432 (PostgreSQL default port) to your application.

3. **Connect Your Flask or Django App to RDS**: Once your RDS instance is up and running, you can connect your Python application to it.

For **Flask**:

   - Install the necessary libraries:

bash

pip install psycopg2-binary

   - In your config.py (or equivalent configuration file), add the database connection settings:

python

```python
import os
from sqlalchemy import create_engine

DB_HOST = os.getenv('DB_HOST', 'your-db-instance-endpoint')
DB_NAME = os.getenv('DB_NAME', 'your-db-name')
DB_USER = os.getenv('DB_USER', 'your-db-username')
DB_PASSWORD = os.getenv('DB_PASSWORD', 'your-db-password')

DATABASE_URL = f"postgresql://{DB_USER}:{DB_PASSWORD}@{DB_HOST}/{DB_NAME}"
engine = create_engine(DATABASE_URL)
```

- Replace the placeholders with your RDS instance details.

For **Django**:

- In your settings.py file, configure the DATABASES setting:

python

```python
DATABASES = {
```

```
'default': {

    'ENGINE': 'django.db.backends.postgresql',

    'NAME': 'your-db-name',

    'USER': 'your-db-username',

    'PASSWORD': 'your-db-password',

    'HOST': 'your-db-instance-endpoint',

    'PORT': '5432',

  }

}
```

- o Replace the placeholders with the actual RDS instance details.

4. **Test the Connection**:

   - o Run your application locally or in your Elastic Beanstalk environment to verify that the application can successfully connect to the RDS database.

Scaling and Monitoring Your Application

One of the major advantages of deploying on AWS is its ability to scale applications automatically as traffic and demand grow. AWS provides several services, including **Elastic Load Balancer (ELB)**, **Auto Scaling**, and

CloudWatch, to help you monitor and scale your application efficiently.

1. Scaling Your Application with ELB and Auto Scaling

Scaling your application involves distributing incoming traffic across multiple instances and ensuring that resources scale based on demand.

- **Elastic Load Balancer (ELB)**: ELB automatically distributes incoming traffic across multiple instances to ensure high availability and fault tolerance.

- **Auto Scaling**: Auto Scaling ensures that the number of instances in your application automatically adjusts based on traffic. This helps you maintain performance while optimizing costs.

Setting Up ELB and Auto Scaling

1. **Create an Auto Scaling Group**:

   o Navigate to **EC2** in the AWS Management Console and select **Auto Scaling Groups**.

   o Create a new Auto Scaling group and specify the desired number of instances, instance types, and configuration.

   o Choose the launch template or configuration for your application.

2. **Configure Load Balancing**:

   o During the Auto Scaling setup, you will have the option to configure an **Application Load Balancer**. This will automatically distribute incoming traffic across your EC2 instances.

3. **Adjust Auto Scaling Settings**:

    o Set scaling policies based on metrics like CPU usage or network traffic. For example, you can configure the Auto Scaling group to add instances when CPU usage exceeds 80% or scale down when it drops below 30%.

4. **Test Scaling**:

    o Simulate high traffic to see how the application scales. AWS will automatically spin up additional EC2 instances and route traffic to them via the Load Balancer.

2. Monitoring Your Application with CloudWatch

Amazon CloudWatch is a monitoring service that provides insights into your application's health and performance. With CloudWatch, you can set up custom metrics, alarms, and dashboards to track the performance of your application.

Setting Up CloudWatch for Monitoring

1. **Create CloudWatch Alarms**:

    o In the AWS Management Console, navigate to **CloudWatch**.

    o Set up alarms to monitor metrics like CPU utilization, memory usage, and disk space for your EC2 instances.

    o For example, create an alarm that triggers when CPU utilization exceeds 80%, prompting AWS to scale up your application.

2. **View CloudWatch Logs**:

   o CloudWatch can also collect and display logs from your application, EC2 instances, or other AWS services. Set up logging to capture errors, warnings, and other important information from your application.

3. **Create Dashboards**:

   o CloudWatch Dashboards allow you to create custom visualizations of your metrics. This can be helpful in identifying trends, such as increased latency or errors, and responding to them proactively.

Deploying your SaaS application on AWS provides a solid foundation for building scalable, resilient, and high-performance applications. With services like **Elastic Beanstalk** for easy deployment, **RDS** for scalable database management, and **Auto Scaling** and **CloudWatch** for monitoring and scaling, AWS makes it easier to manage complex SaaS applications.

By following the steps outlined in this chapter, you'll have a robust deployment process in place, capable of handling traffic spikes and ensuring that your application remains secure, reliable, and responsive. As your SaaS business grows, AWS provides the tools necessary to scale your infrastructure with ease, letting you focus on building new features and delighting your customers.

Chapter 6: Building a Multi-Tenant SaaS App

Multi-tenancy is one of the core concepts in building SaaS applications. It allows a single instance of an application to serve multiple customers (tenants), while maintaining data isolation and privacy for each tenant. Multi-tenancy helps maximize resource utilization and simplifies application management, but it also introduces challenges, particularly when it comes to data isolation, security, and scalability. In this chapter, we will explore the fundamental aspects of multi-tenancy in SaaS applications, how to implement multi-tenant architecture, and the challenges you may face in building a multi-tenant app.

Multi-Tenant Architecture Explained

What is Multi-Tenancy?

In the context of Software as a Service (SaaS), multi-tenancy refers to a software architecture in which a single instance of a software application serves multiple tenants (customers). Each tenant's data is isolated and remains private, yet all tenants share the same software infrastructure.

The fundamental aspect of multi-tenancy is that each tenant shares the same application instance and underlying resources, but their data is separated, ensuring privacy and security. This is different from traditional software models, where each customer gets their own dedicated instance or software version.

For example, in a multi-tenant SaaS application, multiple businesses can use the same application, but their data is kept separate. Users from one business cannot access the data from another, and each business has its own settings and preferences.

Managing Data Isolation and Tenant-Specific Resources

To ensure that tenants' data is isolated, there are multiple approaches that can be employed in the database layer and application layer. The approach you choose depends on your specific needs, including scalability, security, and performance.

One Database vs. Multiple Databases

When designing the database architecture for a multi-tenant application, there are two common models:

1. **Single Database, Shared Schema (One Database)**

   o In this model, all tenants' data resides in a single database. Each tenant's data is typically identified using a tenant identifier (tenant ID) that is associated with each record in the database.

   o **Pros**: This is the most cost-effective and easiest to maintain. It simplifies management because all tenants share the same database instance.

- **Cons**: Data isolation is achieved via the tenant ID, which can lead to performance bottlenecks as the number of tenants grows. It is also more difficult to isolate tenants for backup, restore, or migration tasks.

Example: A SaaS application for project management might have a projects table where each project has a tenant_id column to indicate which company the project belongs to.

- Table: projects
  - project_id | tenant_id | project_name
  - 1 | 101 | "Project A"
  - 2 | 102 | "Project B"
  - 3 | 101 | "Project C"

2. **Separate Databases per Tenant (Multiple Databases)**

   - In this approach, each tenant gets their own database. This provides stronger data isolation because each tenant's data resides in a separate database.

   - **Pros**: Better data isolation, easier backup and restore for individual tenants, and increased performance since each database operates independently.

   - **Cons**: It requires more resources (e.g., databases, storage, and maintenance), and it becomes difficult to manage at scale because you need to handle numerous databases.

Example: Each tenant in your application would have its own database, e.g., tenant_101, tenant_102, tenant_103. Each database is completely independent and hosts that specific tenant's data.

Challenges in Multi-Tenant SaaS

While multi-tenancy provides clear benefits in terms of efficiency and cost-effectiveness, it also introduces several challenges. These challenges need to be addressed during the architecture and development stages to ensure a successful implementation.

1. Security

Security is one of the most critical concerns in multi-tenant applications. Since multiple tenants share the same application instance, it is vital to ensure that one tenant cannot access another tenant's data. Here are some key security considerations:

- **Data Isolation**: Even in a shared database model, ensuring data isolation is essential. Using a tenant identifier (tenant ID) is common, but there must be strict access control to prevent unauthorized access to other tenants' data.

- **Access Control**: Implementing proper authentication and authorization mechanisms, such as role-based access control (RBAC), ensures that users can only access their own data. Additionally, using encryption techniques to store sensitive data is crucial.

- **Example**: **Salesforce** uses a shared database model but isolates data through a unique tenant identifier that ensures customers' data is separated, preventing unauthorized access.

2. Scalability

Multi-tenant SaaS applications must be designed to handle growth. As the number of tenants increases, the system must scale without sacrificing performance.

- **Scaling Database**: With a shared database model, scaling can be challenging. As the number of tenants grows, database queries may slow down due to the high volume of data being processed. Consider using database sharding techniques or implementing read replicas to distribute the load.

- **Horizontal Scaling**: To scale the application effectively, you may need to distribute the application load across multiple servers. This involves load balancing and managing traffic across different instances.

- **Example**: **Netflix**, which handles millions of users, utilizes a highly scalable multi-tenant architecture that separates tenant data using unique identifiers while scaling horizontally to meet demand.

3. Tenant Data Segregation

Tenant data segregation is crucial in a multi-tenant system to ensure that one tenant's data cannot be accessed by another. This applies to both data at rest and data in transit.

- **Data at Rest**: When storing tenant data, encryption is vital. Each tenant's data should be encrypted with their own unique key to ensure privacy.

- **Data in Transit**: When data is sent between the client and the server, it must be encrypted using secure protocols like HTTPS to prevent interception.

- **Example**: **Dropbox** uses multi-tenancy in its cloud storage service and ensures strict data segregation by encrypting files with individual encryption keys per tenant.

Building Multi-Tenant Capabilities

Now that we understand the challenges and the basic principles of multi-tenant architecture, let's dive into the steps you need to take to implement multi-tenancy in your SaaS application.

Steps to Implement Multi-Tenancy in Your App

1. **Define Your Multi-Tenant Model**:
   - Decide whether you will use a shared database model or separate databases per tenant. This decision will affect the way you structure your database, handle scaling, and implement security.

2. **Design a Tenant Identifier**:

- Whether using a shared schema or separate databases, you will need a way to uniquely identify tenants. This is typically done using a **tenant_id** column in your database, which is added to every relevant table (e.g., users, projects, invoices).

3. **Implement Tenant-Specific Logic**:

   - In the application layer, ensure that all queries are filtered by the tenant_id to ensure data isolation.

   - If using a shared database, ensure that every request includes the tenant identifier to query the correct data.

   - If using separate databases, implement logic to select the correct database based on the tenant making the request.

4. **Handle Tenant-Specific Customization**:

   - Your SaaS application may need to allow tenants to customize certain aspects of the application, such as branding, features, and user permissions. Implementing a feature flag or configuration system will enable you to serve tenant-specific settings without complicating the architecture.

5. **Secure Tenant Data**:

   - Ensure that data access is controlled based on tenant identifiers, and implement authentication and authorization strategies, such as role-based access control (RBAC) or attribute-based access control (ABAC), to limit data exposure.

- o Encrypt sensitive data, both in transit and at rest, to maintain confidentiality.

6. **Scale and Monitor**:

- o As your application grows, you will need to scale your multi-tenant system to handle the increasing load. AWS offers a range of services like **Elastic Load Balancer (ELB)** and **Auto Scaling** to manage increased traffic. Cloud databases like **Amazon RDS** offer features like automated backups, scaling, and replicas to handle the growing volume of data.

Example: Implementing Multi-Tenancy with a Shared Database

Let's consider a simple implementation of multi-tenancy using a shared database model. We'll use Python and Flask for the application, with PostgreSQL as the database.

1. **Database Schema**: Create a tenant_id column for all tables.

sql

```sql
CREATE TABLE users (
    id SERIAL PRIMARY KEY,
```

```
    tenant_id INT NOT NULL,

    username VARCHAR(255),

    email VARCHAR(255),

    password VARCHAR(255)

);
```

2. **Filter Queries by Tenant**: Every query made to the database should filter based on the tenant ID. For example, when retrieving a list of users:

python

```python
def get_users(tenant_id):

    return
db.session.query(User).filter_by(tenant_id=tenant_id).all()
```

3. **Secure Routes**: Ensure that all routes are tenant-aware and secure.

python

```python
@app.route('/users')

@jwt_required()

def list_users():

    tenant_id = get_tenant_from_jwt()  # Extract tenant ID
from JWT

    users = get_users(tenant_id)

    return jsonify([user.to_dict() for user in users])
```

This ensures that only users from the same tenant can access each other's data.

Building a multi-tenant SaaS application requires careful planning, especially around data isolation, security, and scalability. By understanding multi-tenant architecture and applying the right tools and strategies, you can create a highly efficient and secure SaaS platform that serves multiple customers while maintaining data privacy. Whether you choose a shared database or separate databases for each tenant, the key is to balance cost-efficiency with security and scalability as your application grows.

Chapter 7: API Development for SaaS

In SaaS applications, APIs (Application Programming Interfaces) serve as the backbone for enabling communication between various systems. APIs are responsible for exposing application features and data to external clients, such as web or mobile applications, while maintaining the integrity of the underlying systems. In this chapter, we will delve into the fundamentals of API development for SaaS applications, including building RESTful APIs, securing them, and implementing techniques such as rate limiting to handle high traffic efficiently.

Building RESTful APIs for SaaS

Introduction to REST Principles

REST (Representational State Transfer) is an architectural style that has become the standard for building APIs. It is based on a set of principles that ensure scalability, simplicity, and performance, making it ideal for SaaS applications that require quick, reliable, and stateless communication between clients and servers.

Key principles of REST include:

1. **Statelessness**: Each request made to the server must contain all the information necessary for the server to understand and process the request. The server does not store any information about the client's state between requests.

2. **Client-Server Architecture**: The client (e.g., a browser or mobile app) and the server (where the data is stored and processed) are independent of each other. They communicate over a network using a standardized protocol (usually HTTP).

3. **Uniform Interface**: The API should have a simple and consistent interface, with standard HTTP methods like GET, POST, PUT, DELETE. This allows clients to interact with the API in a predictable manner.

4. **Resource-Based**: Everything in REST is a resource, which can be identified using URLs (Uniform Resource Locators). These resources can represent objects, data, or services.

5. **Representation**: A client interacts with a resource via its representation. This could be JSON, XML, or other formats. For example, if a client requests data on a user, the server will send back the user's information in a structured format (e.g., JSON).

6. **Stateless Communication**: Each request from the client to the server must be independent. This means that every request must contain all necessary data, and no session information is stored on the server.

These principles allow RESTful APIs to be scalable, stateless, and easy to implement and maintain. Now, let's look at how you can implement a basic RESTful API for user management in a SaaS application.

Example: Building an API for User Management

Let's take a common use case in SaaS applications: user management. The API will allow users to sign up, log in, and update their profiles. This example uses Flask, a lightweight Python web framework, to demonstrate how you can build a RESTful API for user management.

1. **Setting Up Flask**:

Start by installing Flask and creating a simple application:

bash

```
pip install Flask
```

python

```
from flask import Flask, request, jsonify

app = Flask(__name__)


users = []


@app.route('/signup', methods=['POST'])
def signup():
```

```python
    data = request.get_json()

    username = data['username']

    password = data['password']

    if any(user['username'] == username for user in users):

        return jsonify({"message": "Username already
exists"}), 400

    users.append({"username": username, "password":
password})

    return jsonify({"message": "User registered
successfully"}), 201


@app.route('/login', methods=['POST'])

def login():

    data = request.get_json()

    username = data['username']

    password = data['password']

    user = next((user for user in users if user['username'] ==
username), None)

    if user and user['password'] == password:

        return jsonify({"message": "Login successful"}), 200

    return jsonify({"message": "Invalid credentials"}), 401


@app.route('/profile', methods=['PUT'])
```

```python
def update_profile():
    data = request.get_json()

    username = data['username']

    new_password = data['new_password']

    user = next((user for user in users if user['username'] ==
username), None)

    if user:

        user['password'] = new_password

        return jsonify({"message": "Profile updated
successfully"}), 200

    return jsonify({"message": "User not found"}), 404


if __name__ == "__main__":

    app.run(debug=True)
```

In this example:

- The /signup endpoint allows users to register by providing a username and password.

- The /login endpoint authenticates users by verifying their username and password.

- The /profile endpoint allows users to update their password.

Each endpoint adheres to the REST principles by performing operations on resources (users) and returning appropriate responses in JSON format.

Securing Your API

One of the most important aspects of building a SaaS application is ensuring that your APIs are secure. Security helps prevent unauthorized access, protects sensitive user data, and ensures that your API is not misused. Below, we'll discuss the best practices for securing your API, including using authentication mechanisms, managing authorization, and applying rate limiting.

Best Practices for API Security

1. **Authentication**: Authentication is the process of verifying the identity of a user or client. In the context of a RESTful API, the most common authentication methods are:

   o **Basic Authentication**: Involves sending the username and password in the HTTP header. This method is not very secure and is usually replaced by more robust methods such as OAuth or JWT.

   o **OAuth 2.0**: OAuth is a more secure and flexible authentication protocol. It enables third-party applications to securely access resources without needing to expose user credentials. OAuth uses access tokens to authenticate API requests.

   o **JWT (JSON Web Tokens)**: JWT is a popular method for securing APIs in modern web applications. After a user logs in, the server generates a JWT token, which is sent back to the client. The client includes the token in the Authorization header for subsequent requests.

2. **Authorization**: Once the user's identity has been verified, authorization ensures that the authenticated user has the appropriate permissions to access specific resources. For example, a regular user might not be allowed to access admin-only endpoints. Common authorization strategies include:

   - **Role-based Access Control (RBAC)**: RBAC is a system that assigns users roles, and each role has permissions to perform specific actions.

   - **Attribute-based Access Control (ABAC)**: ABAC allows more granular access control by using attributes (e.g., user attributes, resource attributes) to define access permissions.

3. **Encryption**: Always use HTTPS to encrypt data transmitted between the client and the server. HTTPS prevents man-in-the-middle attacks by encrypting the communication channel.

4. **Rate Limiting**: To prevent abuse of your API (e.g., brute-force login attempts or DDoS attacks), you should implement rate limiting. This restricts the number of API calls a user can make in a given period.

Example: Protecting APIs with JWT and OAuth

Here's how you can secure the /login endpoint using JWT:

python

```python
import jwt
import datetime
from flask import Flask, request, jsonify

app = Flask(__name__)

SECRET_KEY = "mysecretkey"

users = [{"username": "user1", "password": "password123"}]

@app.route('/login', methods=['POST'])
def login():
    data = request.get_json()
    username = data['username']
    password = data['password']

    user = next((user for user in users if user['username'] == username), None)
    if user and user['password'] == password:
```

```python
        token = jwt.encode({
            'username': username,
            'exp': datetime.datetime.utcnow() +
datetime.timedelta(hours=1)
        }, SECRET_KEY, algorithm='HS256')
        return jsonify({'token': token}), 200


    return jsonify({"message": "Invalid credentials"}), 401


if __name__ == "__main__":
    app.run(debug=True)
```

In this example, after the user logs in, the server generates a JWT token that contains the username and an expiration time. This token can then be used in subsequent requests to authenticate the user.

OAuth 2.0 Integration

OAuth 2.0 is an authorization framework commonly used in SaaS applications. With OAuth, your API can grant access to third-party applications without exposing user credentials. For example, integrating with Google or Facebook login allows users to authenticate using their existing accounts.

API Rate Limiting and Throttling

Handling high traffic is a critical aspect of SaaS application performance. As more users sign up and interact with your application, the number of API requests increases. Without proper rate limiting, your system could become overwhelmed, leading to performance degradation or downtime.

How to Handle High Traffic in a SaaS Application

Rate limiting and throttling help manage high traffic by controlling how many requests can be made in a given time period. For example, you can limit the number of requests to an API endpoint to 1000 requests per hour for each user.

Example: Implementing API Rate Limiting with AWS API Gateway

AWS API Gateway provides a simple way to implement rate limiting. Here's how you can set up rate limiting for your API:

1. **Create an API in AWS API Gateway**:

    o First, create an API in AWS API Gateway and define the necessary resources and methods (e.g., GET, POST).

2. **Enable Throttling**:

    o Go to the API Gateway dashboard and select the API you've created.

    o Under **Settings**, enable throttling and define the rate limit. For example, set a rate limit of 1000 requests per minute.

3. **Deploy the API**:

- o   After configuring rate limiting, deploy the
      API to ensure the throttling settings are
      active.

In this chapter, we've explored the essentials of API
development for SaaS applications, covering how to build
RESTful APIs, secure them using JWT and OAuth, and
implement rate limiting to handle high traffic efficiently.
APIs are the core of SaaS platforms, enabling seamless
communication and integration with various services. By
following best practices for API design and security, you
can ensure that your SaaS platform remains robust,
scalable, and secure.

Chapter 8: Advanced Topics in SaaS Development

As your SaaS application scales and becomes more complex, you will likely encounter the need for more sophisticated architecture and operational processes. In this chapter, we will explore advanced topics such as **Microservices Architecture, Serverless Architectures with AWS Lambda**, and **DevOps for SaaS**. These concepts are critical for managing complexity, ensuring scalability, and optimizing performance as your SaaS platform grows.

Microservices Architecture

What is Microservices Architecture?

Microservices architecture is a design approach where a large, complex application is broken down into smaller, independent services that communicate over standard protocols (such as HTTP, messaging queues, etc.). Each service in a microservices architecture is responsible for a specific business capability or function and can be developed, deployed, and scaled independently.

Unlike monolithic architectures, where the entire application is built and deployed as a single unit, microservices are modular and distributed. This approach makes it easier to manage large applications, as teams can work on individual services without stepping on each other's toes. It also facilitates scaling, as individual services can be scaled independently based on their resource requirements.

Benefits of Using Microservices for SaaS Applications

Microservices offer several key benefits for SaaS applications, especially as they grow in size and complexity:

1. **Scalability**: Microservices allow for more fine-grained scaling. For instance, if a payment processing service experiences a higher load than the user authentication service, you can scale only the payment service without affecting other parts of the application.

2. **Flexibility in Technology**: Each microservice can be built using the best technology suited for its specific task. For example, a user management service could be built with Python and Flask, while a payment processing service could use Java for better concurrency handling.

3. **Faster Development and Deployment**: Microservices enable smaller teams to work independently on different services. With continuous integration and deployment (CI/CD) practices, each service can be deployed independently, leading to faster iteration and feature releases.

4. **Fault Isolation**: If one service experiences an issue, it does not bring down the entire application. For example, if the user authentication service fails, the payment processing service can still function independently, minimizing the impact of failure.

5. **Easier Maintenance**: Since services are small and focused, they are easier to maintain and update. Teams can work on one service at a time, reducing the risk of unintended side effects when updating or deploying new features.

Example: Decoupling User Management and Payment Processing into Separate Services

Consider a SaaS platform that offers subscription-based services. The platform might have two key components: **User Management** and **Payment Processing**. In a microservices architecture, these two components can be decoupled into separate services, each with its own database and deployment pipeline.

- **User Management Service**: This service is responsible for handling user sign-ups, logins, profile updates, and permissions. It can be built using a Python web framework like Flask and a relational database like PostgreSQL to manage user data.

- **Payment Processing Service**: This service manages the subscription and billing operations, handling payments, invoices, and subscriptions. It might be built using a technology like Java or Node.js, and it could use a payment gateway like Stripe for processing payments.

By decoupling these services, the application can scale both services independently depending on load. If user authentication traffic increases, the **User Management Service** can be scaled up, while the **Payment Processing Service** can remain unaffected.

These services would communicate via APIs or messaging queues, such as AWS SQS or RabbitMQ, ensuring that the user management service and payment processing service can interact seamlessly.

Serverless Architectures with AWS Lambda

What is Serverless Architecture?

Serverless computing is a cloud-native development model where you write and deploy code without managing the underlying infrastructure. Instead of provisioning and managing servers, you simply deploy individual functions (small units of code) to the cloud provider, which handles the scaling, resource allocation, and execution.

AWS Lambda is the most popular serverless computing service, and it allows you to run code in response to events, such as HTTP requests, database changes, or file uploads. Lambda abstracts away infrastructure concerns and enables developers to focus solely on writing application logic.

How Serverless Functions Work

Serverless functions are event-driven and are executed only when triggered. You don't have to worry about provisioning or maintaining servers; AWS automatically scales the execution environment based on the incoming request load.

For example, in an e-commerce SaaS platform, you might use Lambda to process image uploads. When a user uploads a product image, an event (such as an S3 file upload) triggers the Lambda function to resize the image and store it in the appropriate location.

Lambda functions typically have short execution times, typically lasting from a few milliseconds to a few minutes. They are billed based on the number of requests and the duration of execution, making them cost-effective for applications with variable traffic.

When to Use Serverless in SaaS Applications

Serverless architectures are ideal for certain use cases within SaaS applications, such as:

1. **Event-driven workflows**: Serverless is excellent for handling event-driven scenarios where your application responds to events like user activity, file uploads, or database changes.

2. **Short-lived tasks**: Functions that perform simple, short-lived tasks, like sending emails, generating reports, or processing images, are well-suited for serverless architectures.

3. **Rapid scaling**: Serverless is beneficial when you need to scale rapidly without worrying about server provisioning or load balancing. For example, handling burst traffic during flash sales or promotions in a SaaS application.

Example: Replacing Traditional Backend Processing with Lambda Functions

Let's consider a use case in a SaaS platform for processing user-generated content, such as images. Normally, you might have a server-based backend where images are uploaded, processed, and stored. However, with AWS Lambda, you can offload the processing to serverless functions.

1. **Image Upload**: A user uploads an image to an S3 bucket (Amazon's object storage service). This triggers an event that invokes a Lambda function.

2. **Processing**: The Lambda function resizes the image, converts it to different formats (JPEG, PNG), and generates thumbnails.

3. **Storage**: Once processed, the image is saved back into S3 storage in the appropriate folders (e.g., original, resized, thumbnails).

The key benefit here is that the Lambda function runs only when an image is uploaded, so you don't need to provision servers to handle the load. This reduces both costs and operational overhead.

DevOps for SaaS

Introduction to CI/CD and Automation

DevOps is a set of practices and tools aimed at automating and improving the software development and delivery process. In SaaS, DevOps is critical for achieving faster release cycles, ensuring consistency across environments, and minimizing downtime during deployments.

Continuous Integration (CI) involves automatically building and testing the code every time a change is pushed to the repository. This helps ensure that new changes don't break existing functionality.

Continuous Deployment (CD) automates the release process, allowing changes to be deployed automatically to production once they pass tests.

Together, CI/CD forms the foundation of modern DevOps practices, enabling rapid and reliable delivery of software updates.

Example: Automating Deployment Pipelines with AWS CodePipeline

AWS provides a set of services for implementing CI/CD pipelines, including **AWS CodeCommit**, **AWS CodeBuild**, and **AWS CodePipeline**.

- **AWS CodeCommit**: A Git-based version control service that stores your source code.

- **AWS CodeBuild**: A fully managed build service that compiles source code, runs tests, and produces software artifacts.

- **AWS CodePipeline**: A service that automates the release process by defining a series of stages for code deployment (such as build, test, and deploy).

Here's an example of how you can automate the deployment of a Flask-based SaaS app using AWS CodePipeline:

1. **Source Stage**: Code is stored in AWS CodeCommit.

2. **Build Stage**: AWS CodeBuild pulls the code, runs unit tests, and builds the application.

3. **Deploy Stage**: AWS CodePipeline deploys the application to AWS Elastic Beanstalk or EC2 instances.

By automating these stages, you eliminate manual intervention, speed up the deployment process, and ensure that new features and bug fixes are delivered more quickly and reliably.

In this chapter, we've explored advanced architectural and operational techniques for building robust, scalable, and efficient SaaS applications. **Microservices architecture** allows you to decouple application components for greater flexibility and scalability. **Serverless computing** with AWS Lambda offers a cost-effective, scalable alternative to traditional backend systems. Lastly, **DevOps** practices, including CI/CD automation, enable faster, more reliable software delivery.

By leveraging these advanced strategies, you can optimize your SaaS application's performance, scalability, and maintainability, ensuring that it can meet the needs of your growing user base while minimizing operational complexity.

Chapter 9: User Authentication and Authorization

In a SaaS application, one of the most crucial components is the user authentication and authorization system. These systems are responsible for ensuring that only authorized users can access specific features or data in your application. This chapter will walk through how to build user sign-up and sign-in systems using **Amazon Cognito**, implement **role-based access control (RBAC)**, and explain best practices for ensuring secure user authentication in SaaS applications.

Building User Sign-Up and Sign-In Systems

The first step in user management for any SaaS application is creating a reliable and secure sign-up and sign-in process. This involves securely storing user credentials, verifying users during login, and managing authentication tokens for session maintenance.

One of the most common and scalable ways to handle user authentication in AWS-based applications is through **Amazon Cognito**. Amazon Cognito is a fully managed service that simplifies user sign-up, sign-in, and access control, while also enabling you to add social logins (such as Google, Facebook, and Amazon) and integrate with enterprise identity providers via SAML or OpenID Connect.

Using Amazon Cognito for User Management

Amazon Cognito allows you to create and manage user directories, called **user pools**, where you can store user information, such as usernames, emails, and authentication details. It offers several benefits:

- **Built-in user management**: Cognito provides built-in user registration, password management, and multi-factor authentication (MFA).

- **Scalable and secure**: Cognito scales automatically to handle a large number of users while providing built-in security features such as encryption at rest and during transmission.

- **Social logins and federated identities**: Cognito can integrate with social login providers like Google, Facebook, and Amazon, or enterprise identity providers using SAML and OpenID Connect.

Example: Implementing Social Logins (Google, Facebook) Using Cognito

To enable social logins, you must first configure **Cognito User Pools** to support external authentication providers. Below is a high-level overview of how you can enable Google and Facebook login for your SaaS application:

1. **Set up an Amazon Cognito User Pool**:

- Go to the Amazon Cognito console and create a new **User Pool**.

- In the **Federation** section, choose **Identity Providers** and select **Google** and **Facebook**.

2. **Configure Social Logins (Google/Facebook)**:

- You will need to create a developer account with **Google** and **Facebook** to obtain the client ID and secret.

- For Google, go to the Google Developer Console, create a new project, and configure the OAuth 2.0 consent screen and credentials. Similarly, for Facebook, you will create an app via Facebook's developer portal to get the necessary credentials.

- In the Cognito console, paste the client ID and secret from the Google and Facebook developer portals into the respective fields.

3. **Enable the Social Logins in Your App**:

- After configuring the external identity providers, you can integrate them into your application.

- In your app's login page, add the option to log in via Google and Facebook. On click, the app will redirect the user to the social login provider for authentication.

- Once authenticated, the user will be redirected back to your app, where Cognito will handle the rest—creating a user session and returning a valid authentication token.

By following this setup, your users can log in using their Google or Facebook credentials, simplifying the authentication process and offering a seamless login experience.

Role-Based Access Control (RBAC)

Once users are authenticated, the next important step is to control what actions each user can perform within the application. This is where **Role-Based Access Control (RBAC)** comes in. RBAC allows you to manage access rights based on a user's role. For example, in a SaaS application, an **Admin** might have full access to all resources, a **Manager** may have limited access to specific resources, and a **User** may only be able to view their own data.

RBAC is essential for SaaS applications to ensure that users have only the necessary permissions, and it helps to prevent unauthorized access to sensitive data and resources.

How to Manage Different User Roles and Permissions in SaaS

To implement RBAC, you first need to define the roles in your application. Each role will have a set of permissions, which specify what actions the role can perform. For instance:

- **Admin**: Can manage users, view all data, and configure application settings.

- **Manager**: Can manage their team's data, view reports, and perform operational tasks.

- **User**: Can only access their own personal data.

You can manage these roles in Amazon Cognito through **user attributes** or by integrating Cognito with AWS IAM (Identity and Access Management) roles. Based on the user's role, the application will either grant or deny access to various resources.

Example: Implementing RBAC for Admins, Managers, and Users

1. **Define Roles in Cognito**:
    - o Create custom attributes for the roles in the Cognito User Pool (e.g., role: admin, role: manager, role: user).
    - o When users sign up or are created, assign them a specific role based on their job or privileges. This can be done programmatically via the AWS SDK, or through the Cognito console.

2. **Assign Permissions Based on Role**:
    - o You can use AWS Identity and Access Management (IAM) to control access to AWS resources based on user roles. For example, an **Admin** may have access to an S3 bucket containing user data, while a **Manager** may only have access to data pertaining to their team.

- o For custom application permissions, implement role checks in your backend API or application code. For instance, when a user sends a request to an API endpoint, check their role before allowing access to the requested resource.

3. **Example RBAC Implementation in Your App**:

  - o When the user logs in using Cognito, you can retrieve the user's role from their authentication token (JWT) or directly from Cognito.

  - o For example, in a Python-based SaaS application, after the user logs in via Cognito, you might decode the JWT token to check the role. Based on the role, you can restrict access to specific views or actions:

python

```python
import jwt
from flask import request


def check_role():
    # Assuming you have the JWT token from the user session
```

```python
token = request.headers.get('Authorization').split(' ')[1]
decoded_token = jwt.decode(token, verify=False)


role = decoded_token['role']  # Extract the role from the token


if role == 'admin':
    # Grant access to all resources
    pass
elif role == 'manager':
    # Grant limited access to resources
    pass
else:
    # Restrict access for regular users
    pass
```

4. **Protecting Sensitive Endpoints**:

   o For critical actions like creating a new user or accessing sensitive data, ensure that only users with the appropriate role (e.g., admin) can perform them. This can be enforced using role checks in your backend.

python

```python
def create_user():
```

```
if current_user.role != 'admin':

    return "Permission Denied", 403  # Return forbidden
for non-admins

    # Code to create a user
```

By implementing RBAC, you ensure that users only access what they need, thereby enforcing the principle of least privilege and reducing the risk of unauthorized access.

Best Practices for Secure User Authentication

While building a robust authentication and authorization system is key, ensuring that your system remains secure is just as important. Here are some best practices for maintaining secure user authentication:

1. **Use Multi-Factor Authentication (MFA)**:
   - To increase the security of your authentication process, require multi-factor authentication for users. AWS Cognito provides built-in support for MFA, allowing you to enforce the use of a second factor, such as an SMS code or a time-based one-time password (TOTP).

2. **Use Secure Password Storage**:
   - Always store passwords in a hashed and salted format. Never store plain text passwords. Amazon Cognito handles this

automatically, securely hashing and salting passwords when they are created or updated.

3. **Implement Token Expiry and Refresh**:
   - Authentication tokens should have a short lifespan. Implement token expiry (JWT tokens) and use refresh tokens to allow users to stay logged in without requiring them to re-enter their credentials after every session.

4. **Regularly Rotate Secrets and Keys**:
   - Periodically rotate your API keys, OAuth tokens, and other secrets. AWS Secrets Manager or AWS Key Management Service (KMS) can help manage and rotate your secrets securely.

5. **Monitor for Suspicious Activity**:
   - Set up monitoring and alerts for suspicious authentication activities, such as unusual login attempts or IP addresses. AWS CloudWatch and AWS GuardDuty can help detect and alert on suspicious behavior.

In this chapter, we explored the process of implementing user authentication and authorization in a SaaS application using **Amazon Cognito**, including enabling social logins and managing user roles via **Role-Based Access Control (RBAC)**. Secure authentication is fundamental to any SaaS platform, ensuring that only authorized users can access sensitive resources. By following best practices for secure sign-up, sign-in, and role-based access management, you can build a robust and secure system that scales with your application's growth.

Through the use of Cognito, you can offload much of the complexity of user management while leveraging AWS's powerful security infrastructure. Meanwhile, by implementing RBAC, you ensure that different user types have appropriate access to application features, ensuring a streamlined and secure user experience.

Chapter 10: Billing and Monetization in SaaS

Monetization is one of the key pillars of a SaaS business model. It is not enough to just create a great product; you must ensure that your pricing strategy aligns with the value your service offers and is sustainable for your business. This chapter dives into the different subscription models that can be used for SaaS applications, how to integrate payment gateways such as **Stripe** and **PayPal**, and how to manage usage-based billing. We will also explore the real-world examples of successful pricing strategies and give practical tips for integrating and managing billing in your SaaS app.

Subscription Models

A subscription model is the foundation for most SaaS pricing strategies. It provides a recurring stream of revenue, ensuring financial stability and predictability for your business. However, not all subscription models are created equal. Understanding the different types of pricing models will allow you to choose the best one for your target market and value proposition.

Fixed vs. Tiered Pricing Models

The two most common subscription models are **fixed pricing** and **tiered pricing**.

1. **Fixed Pricing**:
   - o In a fixed pricing model, users pay a consistent, unchanging amount for the service, regardless of how much they use or which features they access.
   - o This model is simple to understand and manage. It can be appealing for both customers and SaaS providers because it provides predictable revenue.
   - o For example, a SaaS company may charge $20 per month for their basic service and $50 per month for a premium plan, with all users in the plan receiving the same level of access.

Pros:
   - o Easy for customers to understand.
   - o Simple to manage in terms of accounting and billing.
   - o Predictable revenue.

Cons:
   - o May not capture all of the value provided by the service, especially if some customers use more features than others.
   - o Less flexible in terms of accommodating a wide range of customer needs.

2. **Tiered Pricing**:

   - ○ In a tiered pricing model, customers choose from several different pricing tiers, each offering different levels of service. The tier a customer selects typically correlates to the number of features they can access or the amount of usage they can consume.

   - ○ This model is widely used because it offers flexibility, allowing customers to choose the package that best suits their needs while also enabling businesses to scale and target different market segments.

Example:

   - ○ **Dropbox** uses a tiered pricing model. They offer a free plan with limited storage (2GB), a Plus plan for $9.99/month with 2TB of storage, and a Family plan for $16.99/month with 2TB of storage for up to 6 users.

   - ○ **Zoom** also offers tiered pricing, where a basic free plan allows unlimited one-on-one meetings, but group meetings are capped at 40 minutes. Paid plans include additional features like extended meeting durations, advanced reporting, and more.

Pros:

   - ○ Greater flexibility for customers.

   - ○ Can help you capture more value from customers who need more features.

- Scalable as you can add new tiers as your product evolves.

Cons:

- More complex to manage than fixed pricing.

- May confuse customers if too many options are available.

- Pricing transparency may be reduced.

Real-World Example: Pricing Strategies of Companies Like Zoom and Dropbox

Both **Zoom** and **Dropbox** have successfully implemented tiered pricing models that cater to a wide range of customers.

- **Zoom**:
  - Zoom's pricing model includes free accounts with limited features and several paid tiers (Pro, Business, Enterprise). The model is designed to serve individuals, small businesses, and large enterprises.
  - For instance, their **Pro plan** costs $14.99 per month per host and includes features like unlimited group meetings and cloud recording. Their **Enterprise plan** costs $19.99 per month per host, with additional features such as unlimited cloud storage and advanced user management.

- **Dropbox**:
  - Dropbox's pricing model begins with a **Free plan** (offering 2GB of storage), then moves

to **Plus** and **Family** plans at $9.99/month and $16.99/month, respectively. These plans offer more storage and additional collaborative features.

o The **Dropbox Business** plans offer advanced features for teams, starting at $15 per user per month. The **Enterprise** plan offers custom pricing, tailored to large organizations with specific needs.

Both of these companies' pricing strategies have allowed them to appeal to different segments of the market, from individual users and small businesses to large enterprises.

Integrating Payment Gateways

For a SaaS business, having a reliable and scalable payment system is crucial. Payment gateways like **Stripe** and **PayPal** allow SaaS providers to accept payments securely, while also offering powerful tools to manage subscriptions, invoicing, and customer billing information.

How to Integrate Payment Systems like Stripe or PayPal

Integrating a payment gateway requires setting up the necessary infrastructure to handle transactions securely. Both **Stripe** and **PayPal** provide APIs and SDKs to make the integration process relatively straightforward.

Integrating Stripe for Subscription-Based Billing

Stripe is one of the most popular payment processing systems for SaaS companies due to its developer-friendly API, extensive documentation, and seamless integration with a variety of SaaS products.

1. **Set Up a Stripe Account**:

   - First, sign up for a Stripe account and get your API keys (test and live keys).

2. **Create Subscription Plans**:

   - In the Stripe Dashboard, create your subscription plans (e.g., basic, pro, enterprise) by defining the pricing, billing cycle, and any additional details.

3. **Integrate Stripe API in Your Application**:

   - Use Stripe's API to handle customer payments. The API allows you to create and manage subscriptions, accept payments, and handle failed payments. Here's a simple flow:

   - **Create a Customer**: When a user signs up for your service, you first need to create a customer object in Stripe.

   - **Create a Subscription**: After the customer provides their payment details, you create a subscription based on the selected plan.

python

```python
import stripe
```

```
stripe.api_key = "your_stripe_api_key"

# Create a customer
customer = stripe.Customer.create(
    email="user@example.com",
    source="tok_visa"  # Token generated from the frontend
)

# Create a subscription
subscription = stripe.Subscription.create(
    customer=customer.id,
    items=[{
        "price": "your_price_id"
    }]
)
```

4. **Handle Webhooks for Payment Events**:
   - Use Stripe webhooks to listen for important events such as successful payments, subscription cancellations, or failed payments.

5. **Secure Payment Data**:

- o Make sure to comply with **PCI-DSS** requirements when handling payment data. Stripe helps you with this by not storing sensitive payment information directly on your servers.

Integrating PayPal for Subscription-Based Billing

PayPal is another widely used payment system. Integrating PayPal for subscriptions is slightly different from Stripe in terms of API calls but follows similar concepts.

1. **Set Up a PayPal Account**:

   - o Sign up for a PayPal account and get your API credentials (client ID and secret).

2. **Create Subscription Plans**:

   - o Use PayPal's subscription APIs to create the subscription plans in your PayPal account.

3. **Integrate PayPal API**:

   - o Use the PayPal REST API to integrate PayPal into your SaaS application for creating subscriptions and processing payments.

python

```python
import paypalrestsdk
```

```python
paypalrestsdk.configure({
    "mode": "sandbox",  # Or 'live' for production
    "client_id": "your_client_id",
    "client_secret": "your_client_secret"
})


# Create a subscription
plan = paypalrestsdk.BillingPlan.find('P-XXXX')
agreement = paypalrestsdk.BillingAgreement({
    "name": "Basic Plan Subscription",
    "description": "Monthly subscription for basic plan",
    "start_date": "2023-01-01T00:00:00Z",
    "plan": {
        "id": plan.id
    }
})


if agreement.create():
    print("Agreement created successfully")
```

4. **Monitor Subscription Status**:
   - Similar to Stripe, you can use PayPal's IPN (Instant Payment Notification) or Webhooks

to monitor payment status and subscription changes.

Managing Usage and Billing

For usage-based billing, SaaS businesses charge customers based on the amount of resources they use (e.g., number of users, data storage, or API requests). This model is often used alongside tiered pricing to offer more flexibility and charge based on value delivered.

Tracking Usage and Billing Customers for the Features They Use

To track usage, you need to monitor the customer's activity and record usage data. This can include tracking API calls, storage usage, or even active users.

Example: Building a Usage-Based Billing Model in Python

Imagine you run a file storage SaaS platform where customers are billed based on the amount of data they store. Here's how you could approach the billing:

1. **Track Data Usage**:

   o For each customer, track their file uploads and the total amount of storage used.

2. **Calculate Billing**:

   o For simplicity, let's assume customers are charged $0.10 per GB of storage. If a

customer uses 50GB, their bill would be
$5.00.

3. **Charge for Usage**:

   - You would integrate this logic with your
     payment system (e.g., Stripe or PayPal) to
     charge customers based on their usage.

Choosing the right pricing model and integrating payment
systems are essential to the success of your SaaS
application. By understanding the different subscription
models, such as fixed and tiered pricing, and implementing
robust payment gateways like **Stripe** or **PayPal**, you can
ensure your SaaS application runs smoothly and is able to
scale with the growing needs of your customers. Moreover,
tracking and billing for usage ensures you're capturing all
the value your service provides, giving you the financial
insight to grow your SaaS business effectively.

Chapter 11: Testing and Debugging

In SaaS development, ensuring the reliability, scalability, and functionality of your application is paramount. Testing and debugging are crucial aspects of the software development life cycle. This chapter will explore the various testing techniques used in SaaS development, including unit testing, integration testing, and end-to-end testing. We'll also dive into the importance of debugging, common mistakes in SaaS applications, and how tools like **AWS CloudWatch** can help with identifying and fixing issues.

Testing in SaaS Development

SaaS applications are complex, typically involving multiple components, such as databases, user interfaces, APIs, and third-party integrations. Testing ensures that all these components work as expected under different scenarios, ultimately improving the quality and stability of the product. There are different types of testing, each serving a specific purpose and helping to identify issues at different stages of development.

Unit Testing

Unit testing focuses on testing individual components of the application in isolation, typically at the function or method level. The primary goal of unit tests is to verify that each unit of code performs as intended.

Why Unit Testing is Important for SaaS Applications:

- **Early Bug Detection**: Unit tests help catch bugs in the early stages of development, preventing defects from propagating to later stages of the application.

- **Isolated Testing**: They allow developers to test components independently, which simplifies debugging when things go wrong.

- **Facilitates Refactoring**: Unit tests make it easier to modify or refactor code without fear of breaking other parts of the application.

Real-World Example: Writing Test Cases for APIs Using Pytest

Let's say you are building a **user management API** in your SaaS application using Python and Flask. The API has functions for **creating users**, **updating users**, and **deleting users**. A unit test for the **create user** function might look something like this using the pytest testing framework.

python

```
import pytest

from app import create_user, db, User


# Example: Unit test for the create_user function
```

```python
def test_create_user():
    # Arrange
    user_data = {
        'username': 'testuser',
        'email': 'testuser@example.com',
        'password': 'securepassword'
    }

    # Act
    user = create_user(user_data)

    # Assert
    assert user.username == user_data['username']
    assert user.email == user_data['email']
    assert user.password != user_data['password']  # Assuming password is hashed
    assert db.session.query(User).filter_by(username='testuser').first() is not None
```

In the above test:

- **Arrange**: We set up the data needed for the test (a dictionary with user information).

- **Act**: We call the create_user function with the test data.

- **Assert**: We check that the created user has the correct attributes, and verify that the user is stored in the database.

Pytest is one of the most widely used frameworks for unit testing in Python, and it makes it easy to write simple yet effective tests for various functions or methods in your application.

Integration Testing

While unit testing focuses on individual components, **integration testing** tests how multiple components work together. In SaaS applications, this could involve testing the interaction between the frontend and the backend, or between your application and an external API.

Why Integration Testing is Crucial for SaaS Applications:

- **System Interactions**: It ensures that different parts of the application interact as expected.

- **Third-Party Integrations**: SaaS apps often rely on third-party services (e.g., payment gateways, authentication providers), and integration testing helps ensure that these integrations work seamlessly.

- **End-to-End Workflow**: Integration tests simulate user workflows, helping to confirm that all parts of the system work as expected when combined.

Example: Integration Test for API and Database Interaction

Consider testing the interaction between your **user management API** and a database using Flask and

SQLAlchemy. Here's how an integration test might look using **pytest** and **Flask's testing client**:

python

```
import pytest

from app import app, db, User


# Example: Integration test for API and database
interaction
@pytest.fixture
def client():
    with app.test_client() as client:
        yield client


def test_create_user_integration(client):
    # Arrange
    user_data = {
        'username': 'integration_user',
        'email': 'integration_user@example.com',
        'password': 'integrationpassword'
    }

    # Act: Send a POST request to the /users endpoint
```

```
response = client.post('/users', json=user_data)
```

```
# Assert: Check if the user was created and stored in the
database
```

```
assert response.status_code == 201
```

```
assert
db.session.query(User).filter_by(username='integration_use
r').first() is not None
```

This integration test does the following:

- It sends an HTTP request to create a user via the API.

- It verifies that the response status code is 201 (Created).

- It checks that the user is indeed created in the database.

Integration tests are essential for ensuring the overall flow of the application is functioning correctly.

End-to-End Testing

End-to-end (E2E) testing is the most comprehensive type of testing, designed to test the entire application from the user's perspective. It simulates real-world user behavior and verifies that all components of the system work as intended when connected.

Why End-to-End Testing is Necessary for SaaS Applications:

- **Real-World Scenarios**: It ensures that the app works correctly for real users, covering all major workflows, from sign-up to subscription management.

- **Cross-Browser/Device Testing**: It helps ensure that your application works across different browsers and devices.

- **User Experience (UX)**: It helps identify any usability issues that might affect user satisfaction.

Real-World Example: E2E Testing with Selenium

Selenium is one of the most popular tools for performing E2E tests for web applications. Let's say you want to test the entire flow of a user signing up, logging in, and updating their profile.

Here's a simplified example using **Selenium** with **pytest**:

python

```
from selenium import webdriver
from selenium.webdriver.common.keys import Keys


def test_user_signup():
    # Set up the WebDriver
```

```python
driver = webdriver.Chrome(executable_path='/path/to/chromedriver')

# Navigate to the signup page
driver.get('https://yourapp.com/signup')

# Fill in the signup form
driver.find_element_by_name('username').send_keys('seleniumuser')

driver.find_element_by_name('email').send_keys('seleniumuser@example.com')

driver.find_element_by_name('password').send_keys('password123')

# Submit the form
driver.find_element_by_name('submit').click()

# Assert that the user is redirected to the login page
assert 'Login' in driver.title

driver.quit()
```

This end-to-end test:

- Navigates to the signup page.

- Fills out the user registration form.

- Submits the form and verifies that the user is redirected to the login page.

E2E tests help ensure that all components work together as expected, replicating the full user journey.

Debugging and Error Handling

Even the most well-tested applications will encounter bugs and errors. Debugging is the process of identifying, isolating, and fixing issues in your code, while **error handling** ensures that your application can recover gracefully from unexpected problems.

Common Mistakes in SaaS Apps and How to Avoid Them

1. **Improper Handling of Authentication and Authorization**:

    - **Mistake**: Insecure handling of user credentials, improper session management, and lack of proper permissions for different roles.

    - **Solution**: Use proven authentication frameworks like **JWT** or **OAuth** and ensure secure session management practices.

Implement **role-based access control (RBAC)** to segregate user permissions.

2. **Database Connection Leaks**:

   o **Mistake**: Failure to properly close database connections can lead to memory leaks and poor performance.

   o **Solution**: Always use connection pooling and ensure that connections are closed after they are no longer needed.

3. **Lack of Error Handling in APIs**:

   o **Mistake**: APIs that fail without providing meaningful error messages can confuse users and hinder debugging.

   o **Solution**: Ensure that your APIs return appropriate HTTP status codes and include helpful error messages in the response body.

4. **Scalability Issues**:

   o **Mistake**: Not designing the application to scale as user demand grows.

   o **Solution**: Design for horizontal scalability (e.g., using load balancers and stateless applications). Monitor and optimize performance regularly.

How AWS CloudWatch Helps with Debugging

AWS CloudWatch is a powerful monitoring and observability service that helps you track application logs, metrics, and performance. In the context of debugging, CloudWatch can help in several ways:

1. **Log Aggregation**:

   o CloudWatch aggregates logs from various AWS services (e.g., EC2 instances, Lambda functions, and API Gateway), making it easier to track down errors and anomalies in your application.

2. **Custom Metrics**:

   o You can create custom metrics to monitor the health and performance of your application, such as the number of active users, database queries per second, or the response time of your API.

3. **Alarms**:

   o CloudWatch allows you to set up alarms to notify you when certain thresholds are breached, such as high CPU usage, low disk space, or error rates in your application.

4. **Distributed Tracing with AWS X-Ray**:

   o AWS **X-Ray** integrates with CloudWatch to provide distributed tracing, allowing you to trace requests as they flow through your application. This can help identify bottlenecks or performance issues.

By utilizing **CloudWatch**, you can proactively monitor your application, identify problems, and debug them efficiently.

Testing and debugging are indispensable in the development of any SaaS application. Through unit tests, integration tests, and end-to-end tests, you can ensure that your application works as expected at every stage of development. Additionally, adopting robust debugging practices and using tools like **AWS CloudWatch** for monitoring and troubleshooting will help you maintain a high-quality and stable SaaS product.

By rigorously testing and debugging your application, you can deliver a reliable and smooth user experience, minimizing downtime and providing your customers with the best possible service.

Chapter 12: Maintaining and Updating Your SaaS App

Maintaining and updating a **SaaS** (Software as a Service) application is a crucial part of ensuring its long-term success. As your user base grows and technology evolves, regular maintenance and updates are needed to keep the app reliable, secure, and functional. This chapter delves into software maintenance best practices, including versioning, continuous updates, handling user feedback, and strategies for scaling your SaaS application. We will also discuss how scaling approaches like horizontal and vertical scaling help grow the app's infrastructure to meet increasing demand.

Software Maintenance Best Practices

The rapid pace of change in both user expectations and technology can make maintaining a SaaS application a challenging task. Fortunately, following a set of best practices can make the process smoother and ensure that your application remains stable and competitive.

1. Versioning Your Application

Versioning is one of the most important practices in software maintenance. It helps to manage different versions of your application as you introduce new features or fix bugs. This is essential for both developers and users, ensuring that updates are done in a controlled, structured way.

Why Versioning is Important:

- **Clear Tracking**: Versioning makes it clear what changes have been made over time, which helps when debugging or troubleshooting issues.

- **Backward Compatibility**: It ensures that older versions of the app still function properly with legacy systems, and users don't face disruptions when updating.

- **Efficient Rollbacks**: If an update causes issues, versioning allows you to roll back to a previous stable version without major disruptions.

How to Implement Versioning:

Versioning can be implemented in several ways, with the most common approaches being:

- **Semantic Versioning (SemVer)**: This versioning scheme uses a three-part version number: MAJOR.MINOR.PATCH. For example, 1.2.0 indicates:

    o **MAJOR**: A major change that may break backward compatibility.

- MINOR: New features added in a backward-compatible manner.

- PATCH: Bug fixes and small changes that do not affect backward compatibility.

- **API Versioning**: For SaaS applications that expose APIs, versioning is especially important to manage changes that could break users' integrations. This is commonly done by including the version number in the API's URL, like api/v1/ or api/v2/.

2. Continuous Updates

In the context of SaaS, updates are not just about adding new features; they also involve bug fixes, security patches, performance improvements, and other optimizations. Regular and **continuous updates** ensure that your application is always up-to-date and competitive.

Why Continuous Updates Matter:

- **Security**: Vulnerabilities in software can be exploited by malicious actors. Regular updates help to patch known security issues and prevent breaches.

- **Bug Fixes**: Even with rigorous testing, bugs will inevitably appear after release. Ongoing maintenance ensures that these issues are promptly resolved.

- **User Satisfaction**: Users expect the latest features, improvements, and fixes. Regular updates demonstrate that you care about the user experience.

Implementing Continuous Updates:

To keep your SaaS application updated, it's essential to:

- Use **Continuous Integration (CI)** and **Continuous Deployment (CD)** pipelines. Tools like **Jenkins**, **GitLab CI**, or **AWS CodePipeline** automate the process of integrating new changes into your application, testing them, and deploying them seamlessly to production.

- Monitor user feedback regularly, especially in post-release environments, to address issues promptly.

- Ensure that updates do not disrupt users' access to the app, particularly in live production environments.

3. Handling User Feedback

User feedback is an essential part of the maintenance process. It provides insights into how your SaaS application is performing in the real world and highlights areas that need improvement.

Why User Feedback is Crucial:

- **Discover Usability Issues**: Sometimes, developers miss the mark on the user interface or user experience. Feedback helps identify these problems.

- **Prioritize Features**: Direct feedback allows you to prioritize features or enhancements based on user demand.

- **Improve Retention**: Listening to users and acting on their concerns fosters goodwill and improves retention rates.

How to Handle User Feedback:

- **Feedback Channels**: Create clear and accessible channels for users to provide feedback. This could include in-app surveys, support emails, live chats, or community forums.

- **Categorize Feedback**: Not all feedback is equal. Categorize it into bugs, feature requests, performance issues, or other categories. Prioritize based on severity and impact.

- **Iterate Quickly**: After collecting feedback, aim to iterate and release updates that address the most critical issues. Communicate with users about the changes made based on their suggestions to demonstrate that you're listening.

4. Maintaining Uptime and Handling Migrations

For a SaaS application, **uptime** (the percentage of time your app is up and running) is a key metric. Users expect uninterrupted service, and downtime can lead to customer dissatisfaction and even loss of business. Maintaining uptime and performing migrations (such as database upgrades or infrastructure changes) without downtime is a challenge.

How to Maintain Uptime:

- **Zero-Downtime Deployments**: Use **blue-green deployments** or **canary releases** to ensure that updates are deployed without affecting users. With blue-green deployments, you deploy a new version of the app to a "green" environment while the current version runs in the "blue" environment. Once the new version is verified, traffic is switched

To keep your SaaS application updated, it's essential to:

- Use **Continuous Integration (CI)** and **Continuous Deployment (CD)** pipelines. Tools like **Jenkins, GitLab CI**, or **AWS CodePipeline** automate the process of integrating new changes into your application, testing them, and deploying them seamlessly to production.

- Monitor user feedback regularly, especially in post-release environments, to address issues promptly.

- Ensure that updates do not disrupt users' access to the app, particularly in live production environments.

3. Handling User Feedback

User feedback is an essential part of the maintenance process. It provides insights into how your SaaS application is performing in the real world and highlights areas that need improvement.

Why User Feedback is Crucial:

- **Discover Usability Issues**: Sometimes, developers miss the mark on the user interface or user experience. Feedback helps identify these problems.

- **Prioritize Features**: Direct feedback allows you to prioritize features or enhancements based on user demand.

- **Improve Retention**: Listening to users and acting on their concerns fosters goodwill and improves retention rates.

How to Handle User Feedback:

- **Feedback Channels**: Create clear and accessible channels for users to provide feedback. This could include in-app surveys, support emails, live chats, or community forums.

- **Categorize Feedback**: Not all feedback is equal. Categorize it into bugs, feature requests, performance issues, or other categories. Prioritize based on severity and impact.

- **Iterate Quickly**: After collecting feedback, aim to iterate and release updates that address the most critical issues. Communicate with users about the changes made based on their suggestions to demonstrate that you're listening.

4. Maintaining Uptime and Handling Migrations

For a SaaS application, **uptime** (the percentage of time your app is up and running) is a key metric. Users expect uninterrupted service, and downtime can lead to customer dissatisfaction and even loss of business. Maintaining uptime and performing migrations (such as database upgrades or infrastructure changes) without downtime is a challenge.

How to Maintain Uptime:

- **Zero-Downtime Deployments**: Use **blue-green deployments** or **canary releases** to ensure that updates are deployed without affecting users. With blue-green deployments, you deploy a new version of the app to a "green" environment while the current version runs in the "blue" environment. Once the new version is verified, traffic is switched to the green environment, and the blue one is decommissioned.

- **Automated Rollbacks**: In case of failure during deployment, set up automated rollbacks to ensure that the app reverts to the previous stable version without any user-facing disruptions.

- **Database Migrations**: When upgrading your database schema, ensure that migrations are backward-compatible. Use techniques like **feature flags** to gradually introduce changes to the database and avoid breaking changes during migrations.

Scaling SaaS Applications

As your SaaS application grows, scaling becomes essential to handle the increased number of users and traffic. Proper scaling ensures that your app remains performant and reliable even as demand spikes. There are two primary scaling strategies: **horizontal scaling** and **vertical scaling**.

1. Horizontal Scaling

Horizontal scaling involves adding more instances of resources to your infrastructure. For example, if your application is hosted on AWS, you can spin up additional EC2 instances or containers to distribute the load. This approach is often referred to as **scaling out**.

Benefits of Horizontal Scaling:

- **Scalability**: Horizontal scaling is typically more cost-effective in the long term, as you can scale your application by simply adding more resources.

- **Fault Tolerance**: Multiple instances of your application running in parallel provide fault tolerance. If one instance fails, others can take over the load.

- **Load Balancing**: Load balancing ensures that incoming traffic is distributed evenly across instances, preventing overloading any single server.

Example: Using AWS Auto Scaling for Horizontal Scaling

AWS offers **Auto Scaling** services to manage horizontal scaling. For instance, if you are running an EC2-based application, AWS Auto Scaling automatically adjusts the number of instances based on the traffic load. Here's how it works:

- Define the desired metrics, such as CPU utilization or network traffic, that trigger scaling actions.

- When the metrics reach a certain threshold, Auto Scaling will automatically spin up new EC2 instances.

- When the load decreases, Auto Scaling will terminate unnecessary instances, helping to optimize costs.

python

```python
# Example: Create an Auto Scaling Group with a desired capacity

import boto3
```

```
# Initialize the EC2 Auto Scaling client

autoscaling_client = boto3.client('autoscaling')


# Define the Auto Scaling Group configuration

response = autoscaling_client.create_auto_scaling_group(

    AutoScalingGroupName='MyAutoScalingGroup',

    LaunchConfigurationName='MyLaunchConfig',

    MinSize=1,

    MaxSize=10,

    DesiredCapacity=3,

    AvailabilityZones=['us-east-1a', 'us-east-1b'],

)
```

2. Vertical Scaling

Vertical scaling (also known as **scaling up**) involves increasing the capacity of a single resource, such as upgrading an EC2 instance to a more powerful one or adding more storage to your database.

Benefits of Vertical Scaling:

- **Simple Implementation**: Vertical scaling is straightforward and often easier to implement than horizontal scaling because it involves upgrading existing resources rather than managing multiple instances.

- **Performance**: If your application is CPU-bound or needs more memory, vertical scaling can provide the necessary resources.

Limitations of Vertical Scaling:

- **Resource Limits**: There are physical limits to how much you can scale a single resource. Eventually, you'll need to move to horizontal scaling to handle increasing demand.

- **Single Point of Failure**: Relying on one resource can lead to failure if that resource becomes unavailable.

Which Scaling Strategy to Use?

In many cases, a combination of both horizontal and vertical scaling is used. You can scale vertically for small to moderate increases in traffic and then switch to horizontal scaling as your application needs more resources and fault tolerance.

Maintaining and updating your SaaS application is a continuous process that involves versioning, regular updates, user feedback, and handling migrations with minimal downtime. By implementing best practices in software maintenance, such as **continuous integration**, **user feedback loops**, and **zero-downtime deployments**, you ensure that your application remains reliable and competitive in the long run.

Scaling your SaaS application is equally important as it grows. By understanding the differences between

horizontal scaling and **vertical scaling** and using tools like AWS Auto Scaling, you can ensure that your application can handle increased load and continue to serve your users effectively.

Conclusion

As we conclude this journey into building SaaS applications, it's important to take a moment to reflect on the evolution of **Software as a Service (SaaS)**, the key lessons learned, and what lies ahead. The SaaS model has become one of the most widely adopted paradigms for delivering software to end users, and with the continuous advancements in technology, the future of SaaS and cloud computing is more exciting than ever.

Future of SaaS and Cloud Computing

As cloud computing continues to shape the way we build, deploy, and scale applications, new trends are emerging that are pushing the boundaries of what's possible with SaaS. These innovations will not only enhance the capabilities of SaaS products but will also significantly impact how businesses operate and how users interact with technology.

1. AI and Machine Learning Integration

Artificial Intelligence (AI) and **Machine Learning (ML)** are transforming SaaS products, making them smarter, more intuitive, and capable of delivering deeper insights. The integration of AI is enabling SaaS providers to offer personalized user experiences, automated decision-making, and advanced analytics.

How AI is Revolutionizing SaaS Products:

- **Personalization**: AI can analyze large datasets to identify patterns and trends that allow SaaS products to deliver a personalized experience. For example, streaming services like Netflix or Spotify use AI algorithms to recommend content based on user behavior.

- **Automation**: SaaS platforms are increasingly leveraging AI to automate repetitive tasks, such as customer support (through AI-powered chatbots) or data analysis, which allows businesses to save time and resources.

- **Predictive Analytics**: With AI-powered analytics, SaaS platforms can predict trends and provide businesses with valuable insights, allowing them to make more informed decisions. For example, a SaaS app for customer relationship management (CRM) can use AI to predict customer behavior and help sales teams prioritize leads.

Real-world example: **Salesforce Einstein** is an AI-powered analytics tool built into Salesforce that uses AI to automate tasks, predict customer behaviors, and provide actionable insights. It's revolutionizing the way sales and marketing teams approach their workflows.

AI and SaaS: A Symbiotic Relationship

AI's ability to process vast amounts of data and make decisions faster than humans makes it an ideal companion for SaaS applications, especially as the scale of data grows. It can be used across various SaaS domains, such as customer support, sales, marketing, and even operations, to improve efficiency and performance.

2. Blockchain and SaaS

Blockchain technology has been gaining traction beyond cryptocurrencies, and its integration with SaaS applications is poised to create opportunities for more secure, transparent, and decentralized services.

How Blockchain Enhances SaaS Products:

- **Security and Transparency**: Blockchain's decentralized nature makes it an ideal solution for SaaS applications that need to ensure transparency and security. By using blockchain, businesses can securely record transactions and maintain a tamper-proof ledger, which is especially valuable in industries like finance, supply chain management, and healthcare.

- **Smart Contracts**: Blockchain enables the use of **smart contracts**—self-executing contracts with the terms of the agreement directly written into code. SaaS companies can leverage smart contracts to automate agreements and processes in a decentralized manner.

- **Tokenization**: SaaS businesses could explore the use of blockchain for tokenizing assets or services, providing users with new ways to pay or use their software services, or even enabling decentralized applications (dApps) to be built on top of SaaS platforms.

Real-world example: **IBM's Food Trust Network** uses blockchain to improve transparency in food supply chains, giving consumers access to real-time data on where their food comes from. This technology could be used in other industries as well, improving trust and accountability.

3. Edge Computing and SaaS

Edge computing refers to processing data closer to the source of data generation rather than relying on centralized cloud servers. As IoT devices and other data-heavy systems continue to grow, edge computing is increasingly becoming important for SaaS applications that require low latency and real-time processing.

Why Edge Computing is Important for SaaS:

- **Low Latency**: For SaaS applications that require quick data processing, such as video streaming, gaming, or IoT, edge computing allows for faster response times by reducing the distance between the data source and the computing resources.

- **Cost Efficiency**: By processing data locally rather than in a distant cloud server, SaaS providers can reduce the bandwidth costs and optimize the data flow.

- **Real-Time Decision Making**: Edge computing is critical for applications that rely on real-time data, such as autonomous vehicles or industrial machinery.

Real-world example: **AWS Wavelength** is an edge computing service that brings AWS infrastructure and services to the edge of the 5G network, allowing developers to build applications with ultra-low latency for mobile and connected devices.

Building Your Next SaaS Application

As you now have a strong foundation in SaaS development, cloud computing, Python, and AWS, it's time to consider the future of your projects and ideas. Whether you're building your first SaaS application or refining an existing product, the journey of creating a scalable, efficient, and user-friendly SaaS platform is ongoing.

Here are some key things to keep in mind as you embark on your next SaaS project:

1. Understand Your Users and Their Needs

The best SaaS applications are built with the user in mind. It's crucial to conduct thorough research on your target audience, identify their pain points, and design features that solve real problems. Whether you're creating a tool for small businesses or a platform for enterprise clients, your product must add value and create a seamless experience.

Key Steps in User-Centered Design:

- **User Interviews and Feedback**: Engage with potential users early in the process to gather insights into what they need.

- **Prototyping and Testing**: Build prototypes or MVPs (minimum viable products) to test your ideas before committing to full-scale development.

- **Iterate Based on Feedback**: Continuously improve your product based on feedback from real users. This helps you refine features and ensure you're meeting user expectations.

2. Leverage Cloud Platforms Like AWS

Cloud platforms like **Amazon Web Services (AWS)** provide an extensive range of tools and services that can streamline the development, deployment, and scaling of your SaaS application. With services like EC2, S3, Lambda, RDS, and API Gateway, AWS offers everything you need to build, deploy, and scale a SaaS product.

Best Practices for SaaS on AWS:

- **Use Auto Scaling**: Implement auto-scaling to ensure your application can handle increased traffic without manual intervention.

- **Leverage Managed Services**: Use managed services like **RDS** and **Lambda** to offload the complexities of server management, focusing instead on your application logic.

- **Ensure Security**: Always prioritize security by using services like **IAM** (Identity and Access Management), **Cognito** for user authentication, and **CloudTrail** for auditing.

3. Stay Ahead of the Curve with New Technologies

As the cloud and software landscape evolves, it's essential to stay up to date with emerging trends. Explore how **AI**, **blockchain**, **edge computing**, and other technologies can be integrated into your SaaS applications to provide more value, scalability, and innovation.

Looking Forward:

- **AI and Automation**: Continue exploring how AI can automate repetitive tasks and improve user experiences.

- **Blockchain**: Look for opportunities to leverage blockchain for security, transparency, and decentralized functionalities.

- **Edge Computing**: For applications with real-time requirements, consider integrating edge computing to reduce latency and improve performance.

4. Continuously Improve and Adapt

Building a SaaS application is a dynamic and iterative process. Continuously monitor user feedback, track performance metrics, and keep an eye on your competitors to ensure you're adapting to changing needs and trends. By embracing an agile approach to development and maintenance, you can keep improving your application and adding new features that users love.

Final Words of Encouragement and Resources for Further Learning

Building a SaaS application is a rewarding endeavor that requires creativity, technical expertise, and a deep understanding of user needs. The skills you've learned in this book, from Python programming to cloud deployment and multi-tenancy, are just the beginning of your journey as a SaaS developer.

- **Iterate Based on Feedback**: Continuously improve your product based on feedback from real users. This helps you refine features and ensure you're meeting user expectations.

2. Leverage Cloud Platforms Like AWS

Cloud platforms like **Amazon Web Services (AWS)** provide an extensive range of tools and services that can streamline the development, deployment, and scaling of your SaaS application. With services like EC2, S3, Lambda, RDS, and API Gateway, AWS offers everything you need to build, deploy, and scale a SaaS product.

Best Practices for SaaS on AWS:

- **Use Auto Scaling**: Implement auto-scaling to ensure your application can handle increased traffic without manual intervention.

- **Leverage Managed Services**: Use managed services like **RDS** and **Lambda** to offload the complexities of server management, focusing instead on your application logic.

- **Ensure Security**: Always prioritize security by using services like **IAM** (Identity and Access Management), **Cognito** for user authentication, and **CloudTrail** for auditing.

3. Stay Ahead of the Curve with New Technologies

As the cloud and software landscape evolves, it's essential to stay up to date with emerging trends. Explore how **AI**, **blockchain**, **edge computing**, and other technologies can be integrated into your SaaS applications to provide more value, scalability, and innovation.

Looking Forward:

- **AI and Automation**: Continue exploring how AI can automate repetitive tasks and improve user experiences.

- **Blockchain**: Look for opportunities to leverage blockchain for security, transparency, and decentralized functionalities.

- **Edge Computing**: For applications with real-time requirements, consider integrating edge computing to reduce latency and improve performance.

4. Continuously Improve and Adapt

Building a SaaS application is a dynamic and iterative process. Continuously monitor user feedback, track performance metrics, and keep an eye on your competitors to ensure you're adapting to changing needs and trends. By embracing an agile approach to development and maintenance, you can keep improving your application and adding new features that users love.

Final Words of Encouragement and Resources for Further Learning

Building a SaaS application is a rewarding endeavor that requires creativity, technical expertise, and a deep understanding of user needs. The skills you've learned in this book, from Python programming to cloud deployment and multi-tenancy, are just the beginning of your journey as a SaaS developer.

Keep learning, keep experimenting, and don't be afraid to fail. Each challenge you encounter is an opportunity to grow, and every small success brings you closer to creating an outstanding product.

Here are a few resources for further learning:

- **AWS Training and Certification**: AWS offers free and paid resources to deepen your understanding of cloud technologies.

- **Python Documentation**: The official Python docs are a great resource for learning new features and techniques.

- **Cloud Academy**: For learning about cloud technologies, including AWS, Azure, and Google Cloud.

- **Khan Academy**: A fantastic platform for beginner-to-advanced topics in computer science and programming.

By continuing to learn and adapt, you'll position yourself to take advantage of the latest technologies and trends in the SaaS and cloud computing world. Best of luck in your future SaaS development endeavors!

www.ingramcontent.com/pod-product-compliance
Lightning Source LLC
LaVergne TN
LVHW051345050326
832903LV00031B/3747